Tales from the
Tar Heel Locker Room

Updated and Revised

Ken Rappoport

www.SportsPublishingLLC.com

ISBN: 1-59670-006-8

Publishers: Peter L. Bannon and Joseph J. Bannon Sr.
Senior managing editor: Susan M. Moyer
Acquisitions editor: Mike Pearson
Developmental editor: Noah Amstadter
Art director: K. Jeffrey Higgerson
Dust jacket design: Joseph Brumleve
Interior layout: Kenneth J. O'Brien
Imaging: Kenneth J. O'Brien
Photo editor: Erin Linden-Levy
Media and promotions managers: Kelley Brown (regional),
        Randy Fouts (national), Maurey Williamson (print)

Printed in the United States of America

Sports Publishing L.L.C.
804 North Neil Street
Champaign, IL 61820

Phone: 1-877-424-2665
Fax: 217-363-2073
www.SportsPublishingLLC.com

For my mother, Margie Rappoport,
a shining example for us all.

CONTENTS

PREFACE

Told in anecdotes, stories, and features, this book is a tribute to the phenomenon that is North Carolina basketball. It will be of interest to not only North Carolina fans, but also anyone who loves college basketball or is a sports enthusiast.

Tar Heel basketball is unique, but it is also representative of an American passion. In Carolina, it has been described as a religion. Dean Smith, the Tar Heels' renowned basketball coach, has called the University of North Carolina a special place.

He didn't have to sell me. I had covered college basketball with regularity for most of the seventies as the Associated Press college basketball writer and knew all about the Carolina tradition.

For various projects as an AP and freelance writer, I had the opportunity to interview many Carolina basketball personalities from the very beginning.

I've had the privilege of interviewing a member of the first basketball team, Roy McKnight, chatting with Smith at Carmichael Auditorium in the 1970s, and listening to veteran Tar Heel broadcaster Woody Durham and longtime sports information director Rick Brewer spin Carolina stories from the 1950s to the new millennium.

I have gathered many of their stories for this book, along with others I found in my research, in the hope of showing the evolution of a great sport woven into the heritage of a great university. I had a lot of fun writing these stories. I hope you will enjoy them as much.

ACKNOWLEDGMENTS

After writing two books on Tar Heel sports, I knew just what to expect when I went back to Chapel Hill in the winter of 2002 to research this one: Southern hospitality.

Rick Brewer, the longtime sports information director at Carolina, was gracious and helpful as always. As were Matt Bowers and Steve Kirschner in the North Carolina sports information department, which contributed just about all of the photographs for this book.

As for Rick, I cannot say enough. He gave me his time and many good stories about Carolina basketball, as did broadcaster Woody Durham, the "voice" of the Tar Heels. As I told Rick, he made coming to Carolina just like going home.

As always, I must thank my wife, Bernice, for her editorial and research assistance and her support. No one ever had a better partner.

MEDIA CITATIONS

Following is a list of media sources used in part of my research for *Tales from the Tar Heel Locker Room*:

The Associated Press, *Sports Illustrated*, *The Washington Post*, *Los Angeles Daily News*, *Chicago Tribune*, *San Francisco Chronicle*, *The Wall Street Journal*, *The New York Times*, *The Seattle Times*, *The (Harrisburg) Patriot-News*, *Toronto Star*, *USA Today*, *The Dallas Morning News*, *Chicago Sun-Times*, *Omaha World-Herald*, *The (Raleigh) News & Observer*, *The Orange County Register*, *The Boston Globe*, *The Atlanta Journal-Constitution*, *Las Vegas Review-Journal*, *Newsday*, *The Buffalo News*, *The (Greensboro) News and Record*, *The (New Orleans) Times-Picayune*, *Houston Chronicle*, *St. Louis Post-Dispatch*, *Fort Worth Star-Telegram*, *The (New York) Daily News*, *The (Rock Hill) Herald*, *St. Petersburg Times*, *The Florida Times-Union*, *The Sporting News*, *South Bend Tribune*, *Winston-Salem Journal*, *Austin American-Statesman*, *The (Newark) Star-Ledger*, *The (Cleveland) Plain Dealer*, *(Minneapolis-St. Paul) Star Tribune*, *The Daily Oklahoman*, *The Roanoke Times & World News*, *Los Angeles Times*, *The San Diego Union-Tribune*, *The Baltimore Sun*, *The Tampa Tribune*, *Evansville Courier*, *Ft. Lauderdale Sun-Sentinel*, *Orlando Sentinel*, *The Kansas City Star*, *The Lancaster News*, *Arizona Daily Star*, *(Albany) Times Union*, *Seattle Post-Intelligencer*, *Dayton Daily News*, *Richmond Times-Dispatch*, *The (Jackson) Clarion-Ledger*, *The (Bergen) Record*, *Baton Rouge State Times*, *Tulsa World*, *Milwaukee Journal Sentinel*, *The (Peoria) Journal Star*, and *The Charlotte Observer*.

CHAPTER ONE

The Teens

I t was the fall of 1916 and the "war to end all wars" raged in Europe. On the home front, America was changing from a rural to an urban society. And Henry Ford was revolutionizing auto making and other industries with his introduction of the assembly line.

At North Carolina, the basketball team had its own goal: beat Virginia.

Basketball was still trying to gain a foothold in the athletic scheme at Carolina. One sure way of measuring success was a victory over the Cavaliers, a formidable opponent that had beaten North Carolina seven straight times since the introduction of intercollegiate basketball at Chapel Hill in 1910.

North Carolina was playing under its third coach in seven seasons. Nat Cartmell, the first basketball coach at Chapel Hill, was fired after four years in the midst of a gambling scandal. He was replaced with Charles Doak, who also coached baseball and acted as a game referee. Doak coached the basketball team for two years, and he had some success, but not against Virginia.

Enter Howell Peacock, whose staff started virtually from scratch after a 12-6 season. The coach issued a call for aid from any able-bodied man on campus who wanted to "earn a place on the squad and the training table."

"There were only two lettermen back from the previous season—myself and Carlyle Shepard," said Rabby Tennent. "Peacock soon whipped up a team of fair grade."

But could they beat Virginia? Yes, indeed.

The Tar Heels' 35-24 victory immediately raised the standard of Carolina basketball, which could no longer be dismissed as an athletic stepchild to football.

The Boys from Charlotte

It's hard to believe basketball could take a back seat to any sport at North Carolina. But in the early 1900s, that's exactly how it was. Football and baseball were much more popular then.

"If we had 35 or 40 people out to see a game in those days, it was pretty good," Roy McKnight, a member of North Carolina's first intercollegiate basketball team in 1910, recalled. "There wasn't much enthusiasm for basketball then."

The 1910-11 team was North Carolina's first basketball team. *North Carolina Collection*

The basketball program at Chapel Hill had to start somewhere, however, and because administrators had to give unruly students something to do over the dreary winter months between football and baseball, Tar Heel basketball was born.

Before basketball came on the scene as an intramural activity in 1900, the main winter sport at Chapel Hill appeared to be "rowdyism." Students were openly rebellious, pulling pranks all over campus at will.

"The students once got a horse up to the classroom at the entrance of Old East the night before classes to smell and dirty up the place," recalled Raby Tennent, who played basketball in the early years. "I remember the professor calmly held his class as usual, despite all that mess."

Credit goes to a group of young men from Charlotte for starting up intercollegiate basketball at Carolina.

"The boys from Charlotte just got together one day and started it," remembered McKnight, who had played on a Charlotte high school team the year before. "We practiced outdoors at first because the director of old Bynum Gym didn't want his pretty floor messed up. But we finally went to the administration about it, and he was ordered to let us use the gymnasium."

Nat "Bloody Neck" Cartmell, the Tar Heels' track coach at the time, was called upon to do double duty with the basketball team. The game was rough, more like football than basketball, as McKnight recalled.

"There was hardly anything such as a jump ball. When two men got the ball, they struggled for it fiercely. I [was] flung across the gym by a bigger man many a time."

The schedule consisted of not only other college teams such as Wake Forest, Tennessee, Virginia, and Davidson, but the Durham and Charlotte YMCAs as well. For the record, the Tar Heels' first official game was on January 27, 1911, a 42-21 victory over Virginia Christian. The record for their first season: 7-4.

Not So Scary After All

Imagine playing basketball for a coach named "Bloody Neck." The nickname inspires visions of slasher movies, or at the very least, a bruising Marine boot camp. Actually, Nat "Bloody Neck" Cartmell was not as frightening as he sounded.

"He was grand to get along with, a wonderful fellow," remembered Roy McKnight. "Everybody liked him."

Described as "quiet" and "well behaved," the English track star was brought to Chapel Hill to coach track in 1909 and eventually took charge of North Carolina's first basketball team in 1910. He coached basketball for four years, leading the Tar Heels to a 26-23 overall record before leaving in the wake of a gambling scandal.

Now, about that colorful nickname: His family came from a village in England called Cartmell, and "bloody" was a popular English slang word. "He used the word *bloody*, but it was the worst word I ever heard him say," his wife, Grace, said.

More than likely, the nickname came from a childhood accident, although "Bloody Fingers" would have been more appropriate: He lost two and a half fingers on his right hand when an ax slipped while he was chopping wood.

The Wrong Man

Before taking over North Carolina's first basketball team, Nat "Bloody Neck" Cartmell was a noted international track and field man. At one time he held the world record in the 220-yard dash, and he had won gold, silver, and bronze medals at the 1904 and 1908 Olympics.

One day, he found another use for his running talents, according to a story told by his wife.

Cartmell and his Olympic teammates had traveled to Germany after the 1908 games. While out for a stroll on the streets of Berlin, he got into an argument with a policeman who "thrust himself into [Cartmell's] face and jabbered something," Grace Cartmell recalled.

Cartmell took the policeman's hand, pushed him, and took off like a shot. With Cartmell's sprinter's speed, there was no way that the cop was going to catch up with him, and the English track star was soon out of sight.

Later in the day, police showed up at the hotel where the track team was staying. They found Cartmell, or at least they thought they did.

"They arrested Charles Hollaway, another member of the team who looked very much like Nat," said Grace.

Cartmell hadn't made his way back to the hotel just yet. But when he finally arrived and was informed of what happened, he readily admitted his guilt to the authorities. He apparently didn't make much of an impression.

"They did not believe him, for he was such a quiet, well behaved fellow," Grace said. "And as they had bailed Charlie out already, they left it there."

A Top Lineup

What do a state governor, a general, and a corporation president all have in common?

They once played basketball at North Carolina, and amazingly, they were all on the same team.

It's likely that not many college basketball teams spawned such a distinguished group of government and industry leaders as did the 1916-1917 squad at North Carolina.

That team included a future governor (North Carolina's Luther H. Hodges), the president of an international civic organization (Charles G. Tennent), a corporation president (Elliott C. Grandin), a distinguished lawyer (Bryce Little), a well-known physician (coach Howell Peacock), two research chemists (George Raby Tennent and Frank E. Kendrick), a university professor (John Minor Gwynn), a bank president (William R. Guthberson), two notable business executives (Sidney Curtis Perry and Lewis R. McDuffie), and General F. Carlyle Shepard.

Although that Tar Heel team won only five of nine games, it was significant in that it was the first North Carolina team to beat Virginia, which was quite an accomplishment. That win helped raise the standard of basketball at Chapel Hill from a minor to a major sport.

According to George Tennent, "When you beat Virginia in those days, you more or less had it made."

All Broken up

The renowned 1916-1917 team was invited back for a reunion at a Tar Heel game in 1958. It was just like old times, a bunch of former North Carolina basketball players just hanging together and kicking up their heels. Only this gathering took place in the North Carolina Governor's Mansion in Raleigh.

Eleven of the 14 players showed up, including Governor Luther H. Hodges, a substitute on the team that beat Virginia in 1917, securing its place in Tar Heel basketball history.

Following the game, Hodges received his former teammates at the state capitol. There they relived old times; Hodges recalled having one of his teeth knocked out in a game.

They tossed a basketball around the executive offices. The governor showed off his ball-handling skills, spinning the basketball on his index finger.

Then, suddenly, disaster struck. Hodges flipped an errant pass, and the ball broke a chandelier.

"A wild toss shattered the chandelier and covered the floor with broken glass," George Tennent recalled. "I can remember an attendant in full dress picking up the pieces."

The 1916-1917 team now had something to remember other than their victory over Virginia.

Officially Speaking

It is difficult to imagine a head coach pitching in as a court official for North Carolina games, but that's just what Charles Doak did at North Carolina in the 1915-1916 season. Doak, also the baseball coach at that time, was asked to referee basketball games involving North Carolina, as well as coach the team.

"As basketball increased in interest and the number of games involved became larger, getting qualified referees became a problem," George Tennant remembered.

Doak had to referee several games. The Tar Heels finished with a 12-4 season, their best record to that point. There's no record of how many North Carolina games Doak officiated, but he probably never received a technical from the referee.

Paying Their Way

The 1914-1915 North Carolina Tar Heels had a miserable season under Charles Doak, finishing an atrocious 6-10. But the team was nevertheless distinguished at Chapel Hill.

That season, the Tar Heels nearly paid off all of their expenses. According to *The Daily Tar Heel*, the squad "only" lost $62.98 for the season.

Maybe that is in part due to the players' help in paying the bills. Believe it or not, they had to buy their own shoes and launder their own uniforms, a set of 50-cent gym shirts and shorts.

Catch of the Day

Mixing social activity with basketball in the early days at North Carolina was not uncommon. Once when the Tar Heels traveled to Wake Forest during the 1915-1916 season, a dance had been arranged for them after the game.

George Tennent recalled the "lovely ladies in evening dresses." Partners were decided by the "catch" method, according to Tennent.

"Each lady tossed a red carnation with her name attached down to the players from a balcony. As one sailed my way, the 'catch' was made, and to my surprise, I had the [school] president's daughter, Louise Poteat."

For the North Carolina players, it was much more pleasant than the game, which they lost 27-22.

CHAPTER TWO

The Twenties

I t was the Roaring Twenties in America. Flappers, jazz, and a so-called "Golden Age" of sports. Before the Great Depression ended the decade-long party, it was also a golden age for basketball at North Carolina.

The "White Phantoms," one of the great early North Carolina teams, raced to the 1923-1924 national championship with a 26-0 record. The up-tempo Phantoms, led by Jack "Spratt" Cobb, Cart Carmichael, Monk McDonald, and Bill Dodderer were the early basketball version of the Lakers' Showtime. They had very few close games, usually outscoring opponents by a composite 2-to-1 margin.

"That 1924 team was characterized by quickness and speed," said Norman Shepard, who coached basketball at Carolina for that season alone. "It was a very, very fast team, and we used the fast break effectively."

His best player might have been Carmichael. "Carmichael could drive for the basket with unbelievable speed and hold himself in the air for a long time, like he was suspended," Shepard said. Can anyone say Michael Jordan?

During the Southern Conference playoffs in Atlanta, sportswriters were searching for words to describe the speed with which the Tar Heels played both on both offense and defense. They called the players "shadows and ghosts," and thus coined the nickname "Phantoms."

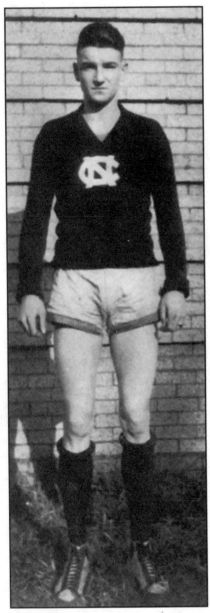

Was Cart Charmichael the 1920s version of Jordan? *North Carolina Collection*

Not to be forgotten were other Tar Heel teams of that decade, starting with the state champions in 1921 and Southern Conference champions in 1922. The old Southern Conference tournament was the forerunner of the Atlantic Coast Conference playoffs and created as much excitement. In fact, it may have been more difficult to win, because it required beating five teams in five days.

"I remember going to the first game in the old Atlanta Auditorium with its high roofs and the fans hanging off the girders," said Dean C. P. (Sally) Miles, who represented Virginia Tech in an organizational meeting of the new Southern tournament in 1921. "People actually fell out of the girders that night."

The Tar Heels also won the Southern Conference tournament title in 1924, 1925, and 1926, highlighting one of the best periods in North Carolina's early basketball history.

Jack of All Trades

In the 1920s, Ty Cobb was in the full flight of a Hall of Fame baseball career. At North Carolina, another Cobb was making a name for himself as well. That was basketball star Jack "Spratt" Cobb.

Cobb could do it all. And he often did, leading the Tar Heels to a 66-10 record and a national championship in his three years at Chapel Hill. While Cart Cartmichael, who also played in that era, was North Carolina's first All-American in any sport, Cobb was known as "Mr. Basketball" at Carolina. He was UNC's first three-time All-American and the Helms National Player of the Year in 1926.

"He was the most graceful player you ever saw," said Curtis "Sis" Perry, who played at North Carolina a couple of years earlier. "Jack never just threw the ball up there. He fully intended to make every shot."

And he nearly did, averaging 15 points a game from 1922 to 1924, while the entire North Carolina team was averaging about 35.

At six foot two, Cobb was a skyscraper for his day, literally head and shoulders above the crowd. He was a ferocious rebounder, a slick passer, and a deadly shooter from his forward position. Cobb was never better than when he played in the Southern Conference tournaments in Atlanta, which he usually dominated.

Cobb didn't have to travel far to attend North Carolina. He was from nearby Durham. After

Mr. Basketball—Jack "Spratt" Cobb.
North Carolina Collection

graduating, he faced a far tougher battle than he ever had on a basketball court. Shortly after leaving school, he was involved in an auto accident and lost part of his left leg. Although a lifelong invalid, he later devoted some of his spare time to coaching Little League baseball. He died in his home in Greenville, North Carolina, in 1966 at the age of 62. Cobb died without the knowledge that he would be elected to the North Carolina Sports Hall of Fame.

Coachless in Carolina

So who needs a coach? Certainly not the 1921-1922 and 1922-1923 Tar Heels, who had a combined record of 30-7 and won the school's first Southern Conference championship in 1922 without a basketball coach. Really.

Bob Fetzer, who coached football and baseball, usually accompanied the team on road trips. During a game, he would go into the stands and watch the proceedings from there. Sometimes he didn't even do that.

Tom Bost Jr., one-time director of Alumni Giving at North Carolina, once recalled, "They took the team up to play at Madison Square Garden [in New York], and Fetzer, who was in charge of them, said he wasn't going to stick around for the game. He told them, 'I'm going to see Paavo Nurmi run. I don't know a thing about basketball. You people just go out there and play.'"

Fortunately, Carolina then had "coaches on the floor," including Monk McDonald, who captained the 1923 North Carolina team and later coached the 1925 squad.

A Change of Plans

Norman Shepard never wanted to make a career out of coaching. He would just do it for a while, until he graduated from law school. At least that's what he thought when he accepted the position of head basketball coach at North Carolina in 1923.

"I decided I'm going to come back and coach and go to law school on the side," recalled Shepard, a three-sport player at North Carolina and one-time minor-league baseball player. "That's what made me make the decision to come back. I hadn't intended to stay in coaching."

The 1924 national championship team. *North Carolina Collection*

But the law career didn't work out. Though he remained at North Carolina for only one year, he led the Tar Heels to a 26-0 record and the 1924 national championship.

He then departed for the Far East to work as a sales manager in China for the Liggett and Meyer tobacco company. It wasn't the first time that Shepard had left America's shores. He had spent three years in the Army, including a year and a half in France during World War I as an artilleryman.

He wasn't finished with basketball, though, and played for and coached the Chinese basketball team in the Far Eastern Olympics.

Having been married at the American legation in China, he returned to the United States after a five-year absence. He was looking for a new career, but instead, he found an old one.

Guilford needed a basketball coach, so Shepard took the job. After filling this position, he coached at Randolph, Davidson, and finally Harvard. He spent 20 years with the Crimson, coaching baseball and football as well as basketball. He retired in 1968, having spent more than 40 years as a coach.

For a man not much interested in the profession, Shepard stayed in the coaching field a little longer than he had planned.

A Flock of Shepards

For coaching achievement within one family, it's hard to beat Norman and Bo Shepard.

Norman Shepard led the Tar Heels to a perfect season in 1924 with a 26-0 record. Bo Shepard followed his older brother in the 1930s with a combined 69-16 record over four years.

They weren't the only Shepard brothers who made an impact on North Carolina's basketball teams. Carlyle and Alex Shepard were Tar Heel players, bringing the grand total of Shepard brothers at Chapel Hill to four. One more and they would have composed the full squad!

"[There were] 500 freshman in my class, and the population of the school was less than 2,000," Norman Shepard recalled once. "[Chapel Hill] was a polished little village and really was a garden spot. It was like one big family. Everybody who went there loved it."

However, he was the only Shepard brother who didn't remain in Chapel Hill after graduation.

It Paid Off

When he graduated from North Carolina in 1925, Monk McDonald received a gift from his father: a scrapbook with newspaper stories of his Tar Heel basketball career.

"I didn't know anything about it until I finished school and was going into medicine," recalled McDonald, who played on North Carolina's national championship team in 1924. "He said, 'Here's something I saved for you. You may not appreciate it much now, but you will later.'"

But McDonald appreciated it sooner than his father expected.

McDonald was working at Presbyterian Medical Center in New York when he got into a conversation with an intern who played football at Tulane, Dr. John Menville. Talk turned to the North Carolina-Tulane basketball game in 1925, which was McDonald's last game at Chapel Hill.

They agreed on the excitement of the game. The only thing they couldn't agree on was the score. The intern insisted he was right and wanted to bet McDonald on it.

"I told him, 'I won't bet you, John. I played in the damn game; I know what it was.' He said, 'In my senior year in high school, I was sitting up there in the stadium, and I think I know what it was, too.'"

There was only one way to settle the argument, and McDonald sent home for the scrapbook.

It turned out that McDonald was right. All of a sudden, he was also $10 richer.

Win One, Lose a Hundred

North Carolina won the 1924 Southern Conference tournament but actually walked away with a financial loss.

The Tar Heels won the prestigious tournament with victories over Kentucky, Vanderbilt, Mississippi State, and Alabama, drawing sellout crowds up to 5,000, twice the size of the student population at North Carolina. But when tournament officials paid partial expenses to all of the visiting teams that came to Atlanta for the popular tourney, Carolina was left with a $100 loss.

Religious Fervor

It was 1924, and there were two notable events going on at the same time in Atlanta—the Southern Conference basketball playoffs and a Bible conference for Baptist ministers.

Some of the ministers decided to sneak away from their laborious conference meetings for some recreation. What better place to go than the Southern Conference playoffs, which featured a superlative North Carolina team?

The ministers were discovered among the animated crowd, cheering on their teams. One Atlanta sportswriter took note of their appearance but decided to be discreet about it.

"We have decided to withhold their names and not give them away to their flocks back home," the writer said.

Wake-up Call

There was no TV then. In fact, there weren't even radio broadcasts of basketball games back to campus. There was only Gooch's Café and Western Union.

Gooch's was a popular campus meeting spot for North Carolina students, who came for the cooking, coffee, and conversation. When the Tar Heels were on the road, it was the spot students gathered to await basketball results from Western Union.

North Carolina was in the finals of the 1924 Southern Conference tournament in Atlanta, and students were patiently hanging around Gooch's to find out the result of the game. The café was packed, even more so than usual.

Finally, word came in: North Carolina had completed a four-game sweep by beating Alabama in the finals. Leading the Tar Heels was Jack Cobb, a Durham resident known at Carolina as "Mr. Basketball."

When news of the victory came in, a rousing cheer arose from the students. The celebration didn't stop there.

An army of students—about 500 in all—marched en masse to Durham, some eight miles away. There they found Cobb's house, woke up the household, and serenaded Cobb's family with fight songs until dawn.

It was probably the only time the Cobbs didn't mind being roused out of a deep sleep and kept up all night by a group of boisterous students.

CHAPTER THREE

The Thirties

Times were tough in America in the wake of the Depression, and the North Carolina basketball team played in an arena that reflected the era. It was a spare steel structure called the Indoor Athletic Court, nicknamed "The Tin Can."

While their stadium was composed only of bare bones, the Tar Heel teams were not. North Carolina turned out one good team after another in the thirties, including a 23-2 squad that won the Southern Conference championship in 1935. Perhaps the best Tar Heel was Jim McCachren, an All-Southern Conference player in 1934, 1935, and 1936.

Defense was the order of the day, with scores such as North Carolina's 31-11 1934 season-opening victory over Wake Forest not uncommon.

"We spent a disproportionate time on defense," coach George "Bo" Shepard said. "We never were blown out badly. If you scored in the high 30s, you had a real good night in those days. Our goal was to keep the other team from scoring 20 points."

From 1932 to 1935 at North Carolina, Shepard had a 69-16 record. Walter Skidmore was another coach who made an impact in that decade at Carolina, going 65-25 from 1936 to 1939 and winning a Southern Conference championship.

Money Players

In four years under Bo Shepard from 1932 to 1935, the Tar Heels never lost more than five games in any season. Maybe it was because of the financial incentives that Shepard created for his players.

"If we won a home game, I gave each player 50 cents," Shepard once recalled. "If we lost it, they got 45 cents."

In those post-Depression years, 50 cents was actually a substantial amount. A player could buy himself a nice meal with the money.

Not that any of them did, as Shepard remembered.

"They'd put the 50 cents in their pocket and maybe buy a snack and a Coke for a few cents, and go to bed."

Splurging

What can you buy for 25 cents today? Not much. But back in the 1930s, it bought you lunch—and left money over for entertainment, believe it or not.

During one trip to New York, Bo Shepard gave his North Carolina players 25 cents apiece for expense money. He told them it was 20 cents for lunch and the other nickel to ride around on the subway.

The 1933-1934 squad dominated in "The Tin Can." *North Carolina Collection*

"If you know how to get your transfers and whatnot, you can ride around on the subway all day long for a nickel," Shepard told his players. "Spread yourself around and have a real big time."

They did.

"We had all these country boys in here, and they thought it was the finest nickel they ever spent," Shepard said.

Tired Heels

The Tar Heels lost only two games in the 1934-1935 season, and they had a pretty good excuse for one of them.

They were on an exhausting road trip in which they played five games in six days. After winning the first four, they were scheduled to travel to West Point to face Army on a Wednesday afternoon.

That night, they slept in the old Pennsylvania Hotel in New York. At least, sleeping had been the plan.

It so happened that Kay Kyser, the famous bandleader and a North Carolina alumnus, was performing in the hotel. He invited the team down to the ballroom to enjoy his orchestra.

"Well, we stayed to about one or two o'clock in the morning, and that was bad, because we had to get up by six or seven," coach Bo Shepard recalled.

To compound the issue, it snowed that morning and traffic was bad all the way to West Point. The exhausted Tar Heels finally straggled into the mess hall about 2 p.m.

"By the time they played, the boys were so tired, they couldn't stand up," Shepard said.

Shepard was particularly anxious for the Tar Heels to have a good showing, because he had been a student at Army just a few years before.

"But we stunk the place out that afternoon," he said. "It was a crime."

Tin Giants

According to coach Bo Shepard, "'The Tin Can' was always freezing. They had icicles in the corner, I remember."

The only source of heat were potbellied stoves and big-wattage bulbs underneath the players' benches. Talk about roughing it; there were no dressing rooms and barely adequate toilet facilities. Players dressed in

Emerson Stadium and made the 300-yard trek to "The Tin Can" to practice or play games.

"We had blankets and wore heavy sweat clothes," Shepard recalled. "Later on they did get central heating in there, but it was never adequate."

It didn't seem to hurt the play of the Tar Heels, who were usually dominant on their home court.

Keeping Wardrobe Expenses down

Like many people in his profession, North Carolina basketball coach Bo Shepard had his superstitions.

"If we won, I always wore the same suit, the same socks, and the same tie," Shepard said. "I washed my socks, of course.

"I always tried to have a blue, a gray, or a brown [suit]. If we won in a brown suit, I'd wear that next time 'till we lost, then switch over. I'd keep the same felt hat all four years."

Shepard didn't have to change much. His teams only lost 16 times in 85 games from 1932 to 1935.

From Ugly Duckling to Swan

Bo Shepard's patience with players was legendary when he coached at North Carolina in the 1930s. Take Jack Glace, one of his all-time "projects."

Glace was six foot four, tall for those days. Though his stature was more than equipped for the game, Glace's basketball skills needed quite a bit of honing.

"He was so awkward that he could hardly walk without tripping over his feet, but he wanted to play basketball so badly, he didn't know what to do," Shepard remembered.

Glace's father was a good friend with the dean of the engineering school at North Carolina. That got Jack Glace into the door. Playing basketball was another matter.

"When he came down here as a freshman, I took one look at him and I didn't think he'd ever play on anybody's basketball team," Shepard said. "The freshman coach worked with him, and the first game he ever got into, he tripped going out on the floor to the referee. It was embarrassing."

But Shepard got Glace to stay in summer school. The two worked out in "The Tin Can," which was as hot in the summer as it was cold in winter.

"We got down there and worked and worked, just he and myself, just down around the basket . . . working on hook shots. That was a favorite back in those days. Then we'd run, run, run downcourt, working on footwork."

Glace played a little in his sophomore season and a bit more as a junior. Then as a senior, Glace actually made All-Conference.

It was one of Shepard's biggest triumphs and one of the main reasons he got into coaching.

"I never did see a boy who loved it more or worked harder at it than he did," Shepard recalled.

A Shepard and His Flock

There were no recruiting budgets and not much coaching help, and yet Bo Shepard somehow turned out winning North Carolina basketball teams in the thirties.

"I never had a full-time assistant the whole time I coached," remembered Shepard, who coached at North Carolina from 1932 to 1935.

Shepard had plenty of players, though, thanks to athletic director Bob Fetzer.

"[He] was a man of vision," Shepard said. "His slogan was athletics for all. He didn't believe in cutting squads."

So when the football season was over, there was a call for basketball players at Chapel Hill in December. Anyone was welcome. Shepard said the best players in that time came from local YMCAs, where basketball was played on a regular basis.

"You'd start with 100, and after a few days, be down to 70," Shepard remembered. "I would end up with 30 on the squad. But I'd see that they got some scrimmage every day just as a kind of reward for coming out and staying. I'd have to concentrate on the first 15, but they all got a bit of attention."

As many as 25 players might be suited up for home games. Shepard would take as many as 15 on the road.

Shepard made the whole thing work, practically all by himself. In his last year, he did have a graduate assistant who was going to law school and worked with the freshmen.

Despite the difficult circumstances, Shepard finished his four-year stint with an .812 winning percentage, the third-best coaching record in North Carolina basketball history.

Bo Shepard's patience with players was legendary, as were his deep-seated superstitions.

An Independent Woman

One Saturday in the middle of winter, Bo Shepard's wife had asked if she could travel on the team bus for a game against Davidson in Charlotte. Shepard told her he wouldn't allow her on the bus.

"In those days, we'd bus down in the morning, and we'd be back after the ballgame, 2, 3, 4 o'clock in the morning," Shepard once recalled. "I wouldn't let my wife travel on the bus because she'd be the only woman, and we didn't want the players to have any inhibitions."

Not only that. It looked like it was going to snow, and Shepard knew it would probably be a pretty rough ride.

The North Carolina team bus took off for Charlotte, without Mrs. Shepard. Some time later, Coach Shepard was at the front gate of the arena watching the crowd come in. To his surprise, he saw his wife and brother strolling toward the entrance.

"My brother was a Davidson man who lived in Chapel Hill," Shepard said.

Shepard had a stack of game tickets in his pocket, but he decided not to offer them to either his wife or brother. "I stood there and said, 'I'll be damned if I'll give them a ticket,' because she had come to the ballgame and I had told her not to come. I watched them pay their money and get on in."

After the game, Shepard walked over to his wife and brother and handed them some unused tickets.

"They didn't think it was cute," Shepard said.

Mrs. Shepard had shelled out 75 cents for the game ticket, but at least she had struck a blow for women's equality. Gloria Steinem would have been proud.

CHAPTER FOUR

The Forties

During a time of uncertainty in a war-torn world, there was nothing uncertain about North Carolina's basketball teams for most of the forties.

Under Bill Lange, the Tar Heels finished with a 23-3 record in 1940 and 19-9 in 1941. The star of these teams was George Glamack, otherwise known as "The Blind Bomber."

A football injury had left Glamack partially blind, yet he was quite able to find the basket. Glamack averaged nearly 21 points a game in his senior year. Remarkably, when he finished college, "The Blind Bomber" was North Carolina's career scoring leader.

When the war stopped, Carolina just kept going. In 1946, the Tar Heels won 30 games and went all the way to the NCAA finals before losing to Oklahoma A&M.

That team featured funnyman Horace "Bones" McKinney and John "Hook" Dillon, whose hook-shot artistry was the talk of Madison Square Garden. McKinney was the Tar Heels' court jester, and his quick wit kept his teammates laughing all of the way to the NCAA Finals.

Coach Ben Carnevale compiled a 52-11 record over two years at North Carolina, followed by Tom Scott, who led compelling North Carolina teams at the end of the decade.

Ben Carnevale coached the Tar Heels for two seasons. *North Carolina Collection*

Believe It or Not

Talk about overcoming a handicap. How about leading your team in scoring despite not being able to see the basket?

George Glamack, "The Blind Bomber," who starred for North Carolina in the early forties, had lost the majority of his eyesight as a result of a football injury.

"I never saw the basket, but I saw the backboard," Glamack said in an interview. "It was so big, and it was so white. I designed a Braille system by watching the black lines on the floor near the basket. I just got to my spot on the floor and shot from there. I took a long time to develop it, but I developed it."

Glamack had an uncanny feel for the court within 15 feet of the basket, according to teammate Lew Hayworth. Glamack was six foot six, big for his time, and hard to move once he got inside.

"He could shoot with either hand," Hayworth said. "He'd have his back to the basket and just pivot. He rolled out and shot . . . the hook shot. He had it down to perfection."

In his senior year, Glamack averaged 20.6 points a game in a time when teams rarely scored in the 60s. He was named to the All-America team in 1940 and 1941, earned the Helms Player of the Year award, and finished as the top career scorer in Tar Heel history.

"I never read the articles about me when I was playing," Glamack said. "I just cut them out and put them away. Then one day I started reminiscing, and I went through all the clippings and I said, 'Oh, my God, did I do that?'"

He was not the only one who found it hard to believe.

Eyeing the Navy

George Glamack tells his story of joining the Navy during World War II despite impaired vision. Glamack had just completed a celebrated basketball career at North Carolina in 1941 when he went before a Navy medical examiner.

"OK, George," the examiner said, "read the eye chart."

"I can't," Glamack said.

"Well, then, perhaps if you got a little closer …"

Glamack pulled his six-foot-six, 200-pound frame out of his chair and walked toward the chart. He missed it and bumped into the wall.

"The doctor told me that wasn't bad at all, and I was a sailor," Glamack said with a chuckle.

Glamack not only was accepted into the Navy, but also played basketball for the Great Lakes station. It was just another mountain

George Glamack, with the ball, was a player teammates looked up to. On the left is Jimmy Howard.

conquered by Glamack, who didn't let a little thing like partial blindness keep him from playing ball.

Sweet Night

When he finished his career at North Carolina in 1941, George Glamack held the top five single-game scoring records for the Tar Heels, including 45 against Clemson.

Glamack had reason to remember the Clemson game for more than just the point total, an amazing feat at the time.

"I was teaching a Sunday School at the First Baptist Church at the time, so I decided to have them as my guests for the Clemson game," Glamack once recalled. "I said to the kids, 'Now, look, you sit there and sit still until I get through. Then we'll go out and have some ice cream if you behave yourselves.'"

That night, Glamack broke the Southern Conference scoring record for a game, falling only five points short of the national record. Afterward, Glamack and his teammates surged into the dressing room to celebrate.

"It was the wildest celebration you ever saw," Glamack said, "and then all of a sudden it dawned on me that I had forgotten all about my kids! I hurried up, showered, and got dressed faster than anything you ever saw in your life."

Glamack was happy to see all 10 of his students calmly waiting for him, safe and sound.

"I was really relieved to see that nothing had happened," Glamack said. "I took them out for ice cream and then I took each and every one of them home."

Apparently Not Impressed Enough

Schools sometimes go to great lengths to lure a basketball player. In George Glamack's case, North Carolina sent no fewer than two coaches up to New York City to meet him at the Stock Exchange. This was in the 1930s.

"I was from Johnstown, Pennsylvania, and Bo Shepard and Billy Carmichael wanted to meet me in New York to talk to me," Glamack once remembered of his meeting with the two. "I'll never forget. It was in a big room in the New York Stock Exchange, and we looked like some executives discussing a big business deal, sitting at a long table with about 100 phones on it. I was impressed."

However, he was not impressed enough to say yes to North Carolina. Glamack, who played both football and basketball, instead chose Duke. Only after problems with the Duke football coach did he decide to eventually transfer to North Carolina.

George Glamack (right) and Hank Pessar do their thing for a publicity shot.

He's Gone, by George

If not for philosophical differences with Duke football coach Wallace Wade, George Glamack never would have become a Tar Heel.

Glamack, who played both football and basketball, was recruited by both schools. He selected Duke, because "I was impressed with the dignity and the architecture of Duke University."

When he arrived on the Duke campus, he fully expected to play football for Wade.

"I had gone to school a week earlier to practice with the team," Glamack once recalled. "One day Wade told me, 'Wear a shirt and tie from now on,' and I didn't go for that. He was one of those conservatives. He wanted everyone to be strict in dressing and so forth. I decided it was too strict for me."

Goodbye, Duke. Hello, North Carolina. And hello to a bunch of Tar Heel scoring records and national honors for Glamack.

Seeing Is Believing

The first basketball player to wear contact lenses may very well have been North Carolina's George Glamack.

Glamack, who had serious vision problems, actually was enrolled at Duke when he was fitted for contacts. The school had sent to Europe to get them. And they weren't cheap at $1,000.

As it turned out, the money was wasted. Glamack had problems keeping the lenses in his eyes.

"They were the size of your eyeballs," Glamack said. "I could only wear them for short periods, and then my eyes started to burn. The university couldn't get over it, after spending all that money. They thought if I could see better, I'd play better but it didn't happen that way."

When Glamack arrived in North Carolina, he didn't need any contact lenses to become an All-American and National Player of the Year.

No Sweat, Orville

Orville Campbell, longtime publisher of *The Chapel Hill Newspaper*, was a North Carolina student in the 1940s when he followed the Tar Heels to New York for a basketball game. The opponent was Fordham, and the place was Madison Square Garden.

Campbell thought he could make an easy five dollars by betting a Fordham fan that George Glamack would score 20 points. Campbell only had "three or four dollars" on him, but it didn't seem to matter. After all, Glamack had been the Tar Heels' scoring leader all season, and 20 would seem to be a lock.

"Well, it was going late into the last minute and Glamack only had 19 points, and, boy, was I sweating," Campbell once recalled. "I didn't know what I was going to do if Glamack didn't get his 20 points."

Finally, with about 20 seconds left, Glamack tossed in a hook shot for 21.

"It saved my life, probably," Campbell said.

Glamack heard about the bet afterward and didn't think that Campell had that much to worry about.

"He was going by past experience," Glamack said. "Hell, if I was a betting man, I would have gone along with his thinking."

Funny Bones

Horace "Bones" McKinney, North Carolina's great center of the 1940s, was a natural-born comic who mixed fun with basketball. It didn't matter if it was just a pickup game, a practice, or the NCAA Finals. "Bones" kept everyone loose.

During the title game against Oklahoma A&M at Madison Square Garden in 1946, McKinney was all over the Aggies' seven-foot star Bob Kurland, mentally as well as physically.

"He rattled Kurland all through the game," Tom Bost of the North Carolina Alumni Association remembered. "He kept talking to him, saying, 'All-American? You're not even All-Madison Square Garden.' He talked to him this way all through the game and flustered him a lot."

Finally, late in the game, the referee called a foul on McKinney. It was his fourth, and McKinney adamantly objected.

"He went over to the referee and said, 'Mr. Ref, the other three fouls were correct. But you missed this one a mile. I didn't touch him. The sad part of this is that I've got another foul in my system, and I'm going to have to commit it. But I figured I had that extra foul to give.'"

Sure enough, McKinney committed his fifth foul with about four minutes left in the game. He was finished for the day.

"He went back to the referee and said, 'You called a good game except for that fourth foul. That was terrible.'"

Not so funny for the Tar Heels was the final score. They lost 43-40. It might have been a different story had McKinney stayed in.

A Religious Experience

It was the 1945-1946 season, and North Carolina's leading scorer was John "Hook" Dillon. The colorful nickname was inspired by an innovative hook shot, although Dillon did not understand what all the fuss was about.

"They said the hook shot was unique for basketball, but I don't know," Dillon said. "To tell you the truth, it was nothing that I developed. It was the only way I could shoot, that's all. They said it was a hook. I took their word for it."

Nevertheless, Dillon won fame far and near, particularly in New York where he had scored 21 points against NYU at Madison Square Garden. In a poll of New York sportswriters, Dillon was voted "one of the most ambidextrous hook-shot artists ever to appear in Madison Square Garden."

Nearly every basketball fan knew about Dillon, even people with seemingly no other sports knowledge. While in New York, Tar Heel coach Ben Carnevale, university controller Billy Carmichael, and Dillon visited Cardinal Francis Spellman.

Upon being introduced to Dillon, Spellman smiled and said, "Yes, I've heard of the 'Hook.'"

Carolina's Court Jester

A funny thing happened to North Carolina on the way to the NCAA Finals in 1946: "Bones" McKinney.

Horace was stuck with this preferred appellation after he played Beau Brummel Bones in a school-play version of *Midsummer Night's Dream*.

"It's better than Horace McKinney," he once said. "That sounds too much like 'Horrors McKinney.'"

McKinney was anything but a horror in actuality. He was a blithe spirit who kept things light on a basketball court. Not that he wasn't serious about the sport—he was one of the main reasons the Tar Heels were one of the nation's top teams in 1945-1946.

"Bones" was born in North Carolina with the appropriate initials—HAM (Horace A. McKinney). As a youngster, his comic talents and love for the spotlight were apparent. Once asked what he wanted to be when he grew up, McKinney answered, "When I grow up, I'm going to be a big boy."

At six foot six, McKinney was actually the biggest player on the Tar Heels. He was also the oldest, owing to wartime service and a previous

Carolina's court jester, Horace "Bones" McKinney.

stint at North Carolina State. In 1946, McKinney at 27 was nearly as old as Tar Heel coach Ben Carnevale.

McKinney tickled teammates with the remark, "Here I am with a wife and a kid, and I'm smoking and hiding from a man just two years older than me."

It was hard for the fans to keep their eyes off McKinney, and not only for his basketball playing ability. They were waiting to see what he might do next—and they were never disappointed in his antics.

Always an actor on the court, McKinney sparred lovingly with referees. When a foul was called on him, McKinney would animatedly "thank" the official. If the foul provoked animosity from the crowd, McKinney would walk over to the official and put his arm around his shoulder. "Don't mind that booing—we all make mistakes," McKinney would say. Often, he would check at the scorer's table after scoring a basket to make sure he was given credit for the shot.

"I always enjoyed playing with him," recalled John "Hook" Dillon of McKinney. "He kept the team loose. He was also very witty, but he didn't clown around when he had to play basketball."

Tale of Two Cities

After leaving North Carolina, "Bones" McKinney played professionally with the Washington Caps of the old Basketball Association of America. And the Durham-born star was always in big demand for speaking engagements.

One of McKinney's typical remarks during a speech:

"Since I became famous, two cities are claiming me— Durham, North Carolina, where I spent most of my life, and Washington D.C. When we blow a game, Durham claims I'm from Washington and Washington claims I'm from Durham."

Southern Exposure

Growing up in Durham, "Bones" McKinney was deeply conscious of his Southern heritage. And the North Carolina star of the forties never failed to invoke it while on speaking engagements after college.

Usually included in his routine was something on the Civil War. Once in Alexandria, Virginia, McKinney addressed the audience as, "Fellow Southerners." He liked to add, "Remember, if there's another War

Between the States, we're a good bet. We were just one mule short in the last one."

McKinney's sense of Southern pride and humor stayed with him well past his college career.

While playing for the pro Washington Caps, McKinney was asked by team owner Mike Uline if he wouldn't mind driving Uline's car to North Carolina and selling it down there. There was a better market for used cars in North Carolina than Washington, Uline insisted.

McKinney was about to accept the invitation but had one question to ask.

"What kind of car do you have, Mr. Uline?"

"It's an almost-new Lincoln," the owner responded.

"Oh, no," McKinney said. "I can't sell a Lincoln in North Carolina. Why, suh, down there, we don't even mention the name."

Follow the Bouncing Ball

After finishing his basketball career at North Carolina in 1946, "Bones" McKinney took his act to the pros with the Washington Caps of the old Basketball Association of America. And it was quite a show.

It's not often that a rookie questions the condition of the basketball during a game. But that's just what McKinney did. Rushing up to referee Pat Kennedy, McKinney shouted, "Get a new ball; this thing is warped!"

Kennedy couldn't believe what he was hearing. But McKinney was insistent. He turned to the fans and pointed to the ball, then rolled it to the other end of the court.

To Kennedy's chagrin, the ball did indeed prove "warped." It bumped along on its uneven path until it finally stopped.

Kennedy had no other choice but to call for a new ball. And the Cap fans had a new hero.

The Wild One

Basketball wasn't "Bones" McKinney's only passion. He also had ambitions to be a pitcher, but his fastball was as wild as his flamboyant personality.

"The hitter and I had one thing in common," he said. "Neither of us knew where my pitch was going."

CHAPTER FIVE

The Fifties

Exploration of space was on most everyone's mind after the Soviet Union launched Sputnik in 1957. That same year, the North Carolina basketball team had gone where no Tar Heel team had gone before, winning the NCAA title. Unlike the Soviets, the Tar Heels took a "railroad" to reach their destination.

Frank McGuire's recruiting technique garnered the nickname "The Underground Railroad." Bringing in many players from his native New York, McGuire's teams had a distinct New York accent.

The core of the undefeated 1957 NCAA champions was from the New York metropolitan area: Lennie Rosenbluth, Bob Cunningham, Tommy Kearns, Joe Quigg, and Pete Brennan. With the help of his contacts, McGuire's railroad later picked up Doug Moe and York Larese, among others, off the New York playgrounds and delivered them to Chapel Hill. They became North Carolina standouts.

One of 13 children, McGuire first wanted to be a policeman just like his father. That was before he was consumed by basketball. He played it on the streets of New York, and then at St. John's, where he also starred in baseball. After a successful high school coaching career, he returned to St. John's as the head basketball coach and led the Redmen to the NCAA finals in 1952. There his team was defeated by Kansas, which featured a fairly anonymous reserve by the name of Dean Smith.

One year later, McGuire replaced Tom Scott as coach at North Carolina, where he had friends from his World War II days. He was given one ultimatum: beat North Carolina State, which had won 14 straight games over the Tar Heels.

McGuire did that in his first season. Then in 1957, he beat everybody.

Wilting the Stilt

North Carolina coach Frank McGuire had a sizable problem when the Tar Heels faced Kansas in the 1957 NCAA Finals: How do you stop seven-foot Wilt Chamberlain?

Tommy Kearns gave Wilt Chamberlain something to think about.

The Jayhawks' Lord High Executioner, known as the "Stilt," was the most feared player in college basketball and had brought his wrath down on many teams that season. His mere presence had a stunning visual impact on opponents, and the Tar Heels simply had no player to match his size and skill.

So McGuire felt that some psychology was in order. When Chamberlain stepped into the midcourt circle for the center jump to start the game, he looked across to shake hands with his opposite number. Or, rather, he looked down.

Standing opposite the Kansas star was none other than Tommy Kearns, the Tar Heels' shortest player at five foot ten. McGuire hoped the move would disorient the Kansas giant. It seemed to do just that.

Years later, McGuire recalled, "I can still see the look of bewilderment and embarrassment on Chamberlain's face as Kearns lined up to jump against him. Wilt looked 10 feet tall towering over Tommy, but they made such a ridiculous picture together that Chamberlain must have felt no bigger than his thumb."

Naturally, Chamberlain outjumped Kearns, but he clearly wasn't the same player that had dominated so many teams. It took the big man nearly five minutes before he found the basket. By then, Carolina had taken a 9-2 lead.

The Tar Heels hung on for 54-53 triple-overtime victory in one of the most exciting championship games in NCAA history. To complete the circle, Kearns had a hand in the end of it, just as he had at the start.

After Joe Quigg made two free throws for a one-point Carolina lead with six seconds left, he deflected a pass toward Chamberlain. The ball went to Kearns.

"I got it and I knew the ceiling was way up there," Kearns said of the huge Kansas City Municipal Auditorium. "I knew there were four or five seconds left, and I knew that if I could get it up high enough, when it came down the game would be over."

New York State of Mind

When Frank McGuire took over as North Carolina basketball coach in 1952, he made no secret of his favorite recruiting territory: New York. And like most New Yorkers, he made no secret of his protective attitude.

"New York is my personal territory," he once said. "Duke can scout in Philadelphia, and North Carolina State can have the whole country. But if anybody wants to move into New York, they need a passport from me."

The so-called "Underground Railroad" connection served McGuire well. In nine years at North Carolina, he had a 164-58 record, including 32-0 in the 1956-1957 national championship season.

Mr. McGuire's Neighborhood

It was New York at its best and worst. It produced such people as heavyweight champion Gene Tunney and Carmine DeSapio, the tough-minded leader of Tammany Hall. It also produced some anti-social types.

"Most of the kids turned out well, but a few turned out not so well," recalled Frank McGuire, North Carolina's basketball coach from 1953 to 1961.

The neighborhood was Greenwich Village, where McGuire grew up and learned the game of basketball.

"He played basketball every day of his childhood and adolescent life—even in driving rain, the snows of New York winters, and the steaming heat of summer," said an acquaintance.

McGuire would work on the New York waterfront during summer vacations. It was quite an education for a young boy who wanted to be a New York cop before turning to sports.

"I grew up on the sidewalks of New York with all kinds of people," McGuire recalled. "You had to get along with them or fight them. We did considerable getting along and considerable fighting."

Going South

How does a tried and true New Yorker wind up coaching basketball in the Deep South? In Frank McGuire's case, it started during the Second World War when he was stationed at the University of North Carolina in the Navy's V-5 training program.

The gregarious McGuire was on a first-name basis with just about everyone in town. From the local barber, McGuire learned of an opening to coach the local high school. So in his off hours, he volunteered his services.

After the war, McGuire's friends at Chapel Hill followed his rise at St. John's (NY), where he led both the basketball and baseball teams to the NCAA Finals.

When basketball coach Tom Scott left North Carolina, McGuire's name continued to show up on lists of candidates for the job. He was soon hired, in 1953.

"Several people recommended McGuire to me, including Ben Carnevale, the one-time North Carolina coach," said former athletic director Chuck Erickson. "McGuire had a lot of supporters."

Case Closed

It was all-out war, a place that separated the men from the boys. The scene was a basketball gym in New York in the 1950s, and the adversaries were aggressive scouts looking to sign players for colleges.

One of the scouts was Harry Gotkin, who had an association with Frank McGuire at North Carolina. Another was Howie Garfinkel, associated with Everett Case at North Carolina State.

They were always at odds, particularly after Gotkin had stolen York Larese from Garfinkel and sent him to North Carolina. Garfinkel had nurtured Larese carefully, but to no avail. Larese became one of the Tar Heels' biggest stars.

Gotkin shared his philosophy on recruiting players. "Look, I just speak to the kid. I talk North Carolina to him. I arrange for the kid to see Carolina's campus at Chapel Hill [one of the prettiest of America's universities].

"I see that he meets some players. Somebody takes him over to Raleigh to see North Carolina State's campus with the railroad running through it. That makes up the kid's mind. He sticks with us."

Next Stop: Chapel Hill

During Frank McGuire's time at North Carolina, a cartoon regarding his famed "Underground Railroad" appeared in the old *New York World Telegram & Sun*. It was authored by Willard Mullin, the legendary sports cartoonist.

It showed basketball players coming out of a New York subway stop on the North Carolina campus. The sign on the subway platform said, "Uptown—Bronx, Downtown—Chapel Hill."

One of the players, carrying a suitcase, was looking at the North Carolina administration building with the thought: "Whatta ya know? The Mason-Dixon line is just an extension of the IRT."

Athletic director Chuck Erickson brought Frank McGuire to North Carolina.

Waking the Near-Dead

Lennie Rosenbluth always seemed to be gravely concerned about his health. His hypochondria was often laughable and led to some amusing moments during North Carolina's run to the NCAA title in 1957.

Once before a game against Wake Forest at Winston-Salem, Rosenbluth developed a coughing fit in the locker room that seemed to get worse with each passing minute. As coach Frank McGuire attempted to deliver last-minute instructions, he was continually interrupted by Rosenbluth's wide range of coughing spasms.

Finally, McGuire stopped talking and put his arm around his star player.

"You're obviously dying," McGuire told Rosenbluth. "Now, I don't want you to die any place but in Chapel Hill. Get dressed, Lennie, and we'll call off the game and drive you home."

McGuire paused.

"My boy, I can't promise you that you will live to see the old school again, but I do promise that you'll have the finest three-day Irish wake in the history of North Carolina."

Suddenly, Rosenbluth's coughing fit magically disappeared. He went out and scored 30 points as the Tar Heels beat the Demon Deacons 69-64.

A Frank Talk

It isn't enough just to put Xs and Os on a blackboard. Basketball coaches have to be part-time psychologists, too. Frank McGuire, for one, was a master at mind maneuvering.

Once before North Carolina's game against South Carolina, Bob Cunningham asked McGuire if he could guard Grady Wallace. Wallace, the nation's leading scorer, had scorched North Carolina for 35 points in their first meeting that season.

"OK," McGuire told Cunningham, "you can play Wallace, but I think he's too good for you, Bobby."

By game time, Cunningham was boiling. He was going to show McGuire just how wrong he was. And he did. Wallace got only three field goals that night, "and two were scored when Bobby wasn't in there," McGuire pointed out. "It was one of the greatest man-to-man defensive exhibitions I've ever seen."

All because of a remark that McGuire had made to Cunningham before the game.

Excuse Me, Coach?

Midway through the 1956-1957 season, the Tar Heels had won their first 16 games, but it looked like that streak was going to end at Maryland. They trailed the Terrapins by six points with a minute to play.

North Carolina coach Frank McGuire had to come up with something to inspire his team. He called a timeout and gathered his players around him, trying to think of words of encouragement.

The words that came out of McGuire's mouth were not what the players wanted to hear.

"Our winning streak had to end sometime, and this looks like it," he told his team. "So, fellows, let's lose graciously. When the gun goes off, go right over and congratulate those Maryland boys."

The reverse psychology worked. Somehow, the Tar Heels found a way to tie the score in regulation. They finally won in double overtime 65-61 to extend their winning streak to 17.

Practice, Practice, Practice

Few basketball teams were as well prepared for games as Frank McGuire's. Practices usually lasted about two hours, and every conceivable type of game situation was addressed.

"When we were forced into overtime games, the boys knew what had to be done," McGuire said.

Against South Carolina early in the 1956-1957 season, the Tar Heels' theoretical practices paid off. The Tar Heels trailed by three points with 40 seconds left in overtime.

Stanley Groll, the eighth man on the North Carolina squad, picked off a rebound. Instead of trying to put the ball through the hoop, Groll faked a shot.

Practically the entire South Carolina team went up to block it, but Groll dribbled back to the foul line and passed to Tommy Kearns. The North Carolina guard drove in, scored, and was fouled on the play. He made the free throw for a three-point play that North Carolina needed to tie the game. The Tar Heels went on to win.

"The play was executed under the most heated game conditions, exactly as we had practiced it in our own gym," McGuire said.

A Promise Is a Promise

Lennie Rosenbluth was the brightest star of North Carolina's national championship team in 1957. Bringing him to Chapel Hill required a total team effort, including a sacrifice by Rosenbluth's mother.

Frank McGuire got the word about this hot New York prospect from scout Harry Gotkin, who insisted that North Carolina grab him in a hurry. There was only one problem: Rosenbluth's high school grades weren't quite good enough.

Gotkin convinced Rosenbluth's mother that if her son had better grades, he could go to North Carolina. Mrs. Rosenbluth was sold on the university. So much so that she hocked $800 of her furs to send her son to Staunton Military Academy in Virginia.

With Rosenbluth starring at Staunton, college offers from around the country began to pile up. He could have gone almost anywhere but decided on North Carolina out of loyalty. "We made a promise to Mr. Gotkin, and he made a promise to me," Mrs. Rosenbluth said.

Lennie Rosenbluth was the perfect player for a perfect team.

McGuire's Miracle

The Tar Heels were enjoying an unbeaten season in 1956-1957. Well, almost everyone was enjoying it.

"The pressure was tremendous," coach Frank McGuire recalled. "It was similar to a pitcher nearing a no-hitter in baseball."

As the Tar Heels' winning streak continued, a nervous McGuire would hear about it everywhere he went in town.

Frank McGuire (right), with Lee Shaffer, found a way to beat North Carolina State—and then everyone else!

"I would walk into the barber shop and somebody would say, 'Frank, I think your team will go all the way.' Why, that was ridiculous, and I told them so. We had won 15 or 16 games then. We had to get by Wake Forest two more times, Duke twice, South Carolina and North Carolina State again, and then play in the conference tournament. It would keep me awake at night, thinking about all those people so ignorant about basketball that they thought we could go all the way."

Making matters worse were the well-meaning fans. Strangers would walk up to McGuire and slip him a nutmeg, a lucky coin, or even a rabbit's foot to carry in his pocket. One student thought he would jinx the team if he moved his car. So he let it stand where it was and collect parking tickets until the season was over.

McGuire was at home the morning after the big victory over North Carolina State, the Tar Heels' 15th straight win. Patsy, his 15-year-old daughter, burst into the room with a newspaper.

"Daddy, you're number one! You're number one!"

McGuire was happy—but not for long. From the other room, 10-year-old Carol Ann, his other daughter, caustically piped up:

"There's only one way to go now, Daddy, isn't there?"

Ultimately, McGuire's Tar Heels finished with a 32-0 record and the national championship. No one was more relieved than McGuire. One perfect season was enough as far as he was concerned.

"I thought for sure we would lose at least four games we won, and finally I almost hoped we would get beaten just to take the terrific pressure off the players. Well, not the players so much, because they kept cool even if I didn't."

Making No Bones About It

The streaking Tar Heels of 1956-1957 pretty much reflected the chip-on-the-shoulder swagger of New Yorkers. Of course, many of them were.

"Everyone was waiting for them to crack, but these kids wouldn't," recalled coach Frank McGuire. "The players seemed to take the pressure far better than the fans or I did."

Late in the season, the Tar Heels were playing in the Atlantic Coast Conference playoffs. No one had beaten them yet, but Wake Forest was giving it a good try.

Pete Brennan was on the foul line for the Tar Heels, and the pressure was mounting. Over the noise of the crowd at Wake Forest's Reynolds Coliseum came a booming voice from the Demon Deacon bench, "Don't choke, Brennan!" It was "Bones" McKinney, the former North Carolina player who was now an assistant coach with the Demon Deacons.

Brennan calmly sank the shot, and then made sure he passed by the Wake Forest bench on his trip down the court.

"How's that for choking, 'Bones'?" he shouted at McKinney.

Kicking up His Heels

"Bones" McKinney, probably the funniest man who ever wore a North Carolina basketball uniform, was never short of story material. Some of the stories were even true.

McKinney, also a successful coach, had brought his Wake Forest team to Lexington for a tournament. He was sitting at the end of the bench, animated as usual with his long arms and legs flying in different directions with the ebb and flow of the action.

One time, McKinney kicked his leg so high that a shoe went flying out to beyond the top of the foul circle. Luckily, the teams were playing at the other end at the time.

He went out to get his shoe, bent over, and dropped a few things on the court. Now he was down on his hands and knees.

"All of a sudden, I looked up and here they come in a fast break," McKinney recalled.

What did he do?

"Just dropped back and started playing defense."

Open Invitation

Luther Hodges was never at a loss for words, but this time the North Carolina governor was having a hard time getting a word in edgewise. The occasion was a wild celebration for the Tar Heels, who had just returned home from their victory over Kansas in the 1957 NCAA Finals.

A lively crowd estimated at 10,000 had greeted the team's arrival at the Raleigh-Durham Airport. The fans picked up players and carried them on their shoulders down the airport ramp.

The impromptu celebration spoiled plans of a formal homecoming featuring Hodges, a former Tar Heel player, as one of the speakers. While the fans cheered and frolicked, the sedate Hodges attempted time and again to give his welcome-home speech.

He sputtered and stuttered for a while, then finally gave up.

"Aw, shucks, you boys come over to the Governor's Mansion for supper anytime you want," Hodges finally said.

How Times Have Changed

No question, the Final Four is the hottest ticket in college basketball, maybe in all of sports. But Dean Smith remembers when it wasn't.

He was a reserve guard on the Kansas team that won the national championship in 1952. Recalling his first Final Four in Seattle, Smith said, "They gave us [each] two tickets, and we couldn't get rid of them."

These days, just try to get a ticket to the championship round—unless you want to pay thousands of dollars to scalpers.

Opening the Door

It was 1959, a year before the celebrated sit-in by blacks at a Woolworth's in Greensboro, North Carolina. And some time before a social revolution would completely change America, particularly in the South.

Dean Smith was 28 then, an assistant basketball coach at North Carolina and a member of the local Baptist church. The church pastor, Robert Seymour, needed assistance from Smith on a sensitive issue. Would he help open some doors for a visiting black theological student? First mission: a popular local restaurant where blacks were most certainly not welcome, The Pines.

"I told Dean that if he came with us to the restaurant, I was almost certain we would be served," Seymour said. "He was eager to do it."

The party of three entered the restaurant, sat down, and had a meal without so much as a word from the restaurant staff. Mission accomplished.

It would not be the only time that Smith would help to break the color barrier at North Carolina. In 1966, when he was head coach, he brought Charlie Scott to Chapel Hill as the first black basketball player in the school's history.

To Sir, with the Basketball

Coaching basketball at a military academy in the 1950s presented a unique challenge for Dean Smith. The players at the Air Force Academy were too disciplined for their own good, he recalled.

"The boys were so well trained, they marched to class, and the freshmen ate at attention and everything, and on the basketball court they'd call you 'sir.' That was fine, but when it reached the point where they said, 'Pass the ball, sir,' that was taking it too far."

Appreciating Loyalty

Dean Smith was one of many coaches attending the 1957 NCAA Finals in Kansas City. It wasn't just another game for Smith, who was rooting for his alma mater Kansas against North Carolina.

Smith, the assistant coach at the Air Force Academy then under Bob Spear, would be rooming with his boss and two other coaches in a hotel suite.

One of the coaches happened to be Frank McGuire, who was coaching the Tar Heels. The other was Ben Carnevale, the Navy coach who was a friend to both McGuire and Spear.

Aware of Smith's allegiance to Kansas, where he had played on the national championship team in 1952 and also coached there, McGuire couldn't resist asking, "Who are you pulling for, us or Kansas?"

"Kansas, that's my alma mater," Smith responded.

McGuire just grinned and said, "That's true loyalty for you."

The next morning, after North Carolina had beaten Kansas, Smith was having breakfast with McGuire.

"He asked me then if I would be interested in joining him as an assistant coach, in the event an opening existed," Smith recalled. "My answer was yes, for I knew it would be a great privilege to serve under this fine coach."

Smith didn't hear from McGuire for a year. By that time, McGuire's top assistant Buck Freeman had left and the offer to Smith was still on the table. Smith felt he knew why. It all had to do with a little give and take with McGuire about rooting interest at the previous year's finals.

"Somehow, I feel this loyalty to Kansas paved the way for my coming to Chapel Hill," Smith said.

Wish You Were Here

It was one of the wildest victory celebrations anyone could remember. Some 10,000 fans stormed the Raleigh-Durham airport to welcome home North Carolina's national champions in 1957. Talk about a full-court press.

Just about everyone was there—with the exception of the Tar Heels' top player, Lennie Rosenbluth.

Where was Lennie? In New York, to appear on Ed Sullivan's television show honoring the first-team All-Americans that year. Years later, Rosenbluth still expressed misgivings that he missed the Tar Heel celebration.

By the way, standing on Sullivan's stage with Rosenbluth was none other than Wilt Chamberlain of Kansas, the team that North Carolina had beaten in triple overtime for the title. Other All-Americans honored that year: Rod Hundley of West Virginia, Gary Thompson of Iowa State, and Chet Forte of Columbia.

Tuned In

Talk about excitement, few teams generated it like Frank McGuire's NCAA champions of 1957. Most everyone in the state of North Carolina was following the Tar Heels that year. Could they actually go through the season undefeated? Would they win the national championship?

"People who weren't basketball fans suddenly were fans and got really caught up in it," remembered Woody Durham, the longtime Tar Heel broadcaster. "It was like a brushfire across the state."

Durham was in high school during McGuire's "miracle season" and a fierce Tar Heel fan himself. One night, Durham and his friends were attending a high school basketball game when someone walked in and said it looked like Carolina was about to lose to Maryland.

Suddenly, high school loyalty took a back seat to Tar Heel loyalty. Woody remembered:

"Practically everybody left the gym, went out to their cars, started the engines, and put the radios on to listen."

The vibes must have been good for the Tar Heels. They came back to win in overtime, continuing their streak. They finished a 32-0 season with a victory over Kansas for the national championship.

One Strike Against North Carolina State

If not for a teachers' strike in New York, it's a cinch that North Carolina would not have won the NCAA title in 1957.

What does a teachers' strike in New York have to do with a basketball team in North Carolina? Plenty, according to a story told by Lennie Rosenbluth to Tar Heel broadcaster Woody Durham.

At the time, Harry Gotkin was recruiting New York talent for Everett Case at North Carolina State. Rosenbluth was one of the top high school players in New York, and Gotkin asked Case to take a look at him.

There was only one problem: The teachers' strike in the city had halted the basketball season, and Rosenbluth hadn't been playing much.

"He was so out of shape, he was winded, and Case didn't like him," Durham said. "He told Gotkin he wasn't going to take him.

"According to Lenny, Gotkin got mad and called Frank McGuire. He said he would start getting him New York talent. He knew McGuire was going south, either to North Carolina or Alabama."

McGuire, who had left St. John's in New York, wound up at North Carolina. And Rosenbluth eventually did, too. He became the Tar Heels' top scorer, leading them to their perfect season in 1956-1957.

Hail the Conquering Hero

As a senior, North Carolina's Pete Brennan shared first-team All-America honors with no less than Wilt Chamberlain, Elgin Baylor, Oscar Robertson, and Guy Rodgers.

He's probably better remembered at North Carolina for a single shot he made against Michigan State in his junior year. Just about everyone knew about it with the exception of one woman in a Brooklyn tenement building.

It was the national semifinals in 1957, and North Carolina trailed Michigan State 64-62 with 11 seconds left in the first overtime period. Johnny Green, the high-jumping Spartan star, was at the free throw line, and it looked like it was all over for Carolina.

But Green missed the foul shot, and Brennan snared the rebound. Instead of throwing the outlet pass to a guard as he normally would, Brennan took off downcourt with the ball. Two Michigan State players were back to defend, so Brennan pulled up at the foul line and hit a jumper to send the game into a second overtime.

The Tar Heels eventually won 74-70 in triple overtime and then beat Kansas and Chamberlain for the national title in another triple-overtime dandy.

Brennan went home to visit his family after that remarkable weekend. Carrying his suitcase up the front stairs of the Brooklyn tenement that he lived in with nine brothers and sisters, he was ready to be greeted as a returning hero. Apparently, one woman who lived in the apartment house knew nothing about basketball.

Leaning out of her apartment window, she called out:

"Hey, everybody. Come look! Petey's home from the service."

Lucky Wheels

Good luck charms come in all shapes and sizes. Some have a lucky rabbit's foot; Pete Brennan and the North Carolina Tar Heels had their "lucky car."

Before the 1956-1957 basketball season, Brennan had brought his battered old Buick to the campus and parked it right in front of the Monogram Club. The only problem was that it was a no-parking zone.

Brennan didn't worry about it much. He merely left a note on the car addressed to campus police that he would move the vehicle eventually.

Probably because Brennan was a player on a winning basketball team, the police gave him a little more slack than they would have other students.

Weeks passed, then months, and the police continued to nudge Brennan gently to move the vehicle. But he was too busy helping the Tar Heels win games to worry about the car.

And the Tar Heels were really on a run. They hadn't lost a game yet. After a while, everyone on campus (police included) believed that moving the car would be bad luck. Brennan promised he would move the car once the Tar Heels lost their first game.

It never happened. They finished the season with a 32-0 record and won the NCAA championship in the process. And Brennan's car was accorded its legendary status as a good-luck charm.

The story has a postcript. Actually, the car was moved during the season—as a prank by North Carolina State students, who had heard about Carolina's so-called lucky car. They also swabbed it with red paint, the Wolfpack's primary color.

Actually, it was a lucky break for Brennan. The State students had moved the car into a legal parking spot.

Pete Brennan was the owner of the "Lucky Wheels."

Taken to the Cleaners

Basketball coaches have been known to be a pretty superstitious breed. A dry-cleaning man in Chapel Hill helped to start a new tradition for North Carolina coach Frank McGuire.

It was the day of an important game with North Carolina State during the 1954-1955 season when the doorbell rang at McGuire's house.

Who would be calling at 8 a.m., McGuire wondered? It was Ruie Ewbanks, Sr., who was employed by the Cheek Dry Cleaners.

"Coach, I want to apologize for calling on you so early, but I want you to win that game [against North Carolina State] badly," Ewbanks said. "On two other occasions I picked up dry cleaning from you on the days of important games, and, by George, you won. That's why I'm here today."

McGuire said sorry, he had no clothes for the cleaner that day. But, on second thought, maybe he would try to scrape up something just in case. McGuire excused himself and soon came back with a sport coat and shirt.

He thanked the cleaning man for his support and went about his business preparing for the Wolfpack, who were heavily favored to beat the Tar Heels. North Carolina State had the national ranking and the home court advantage, but neither of those things seemed to matter as North Carolina pulled off an 84-80 upset at the Reynolds Coliseum.

From that day on, McGuire promised that any time the dry cleaning man showed up at his door, he would find something to give him.

Ready When You Are, C.D.

It was the dark ages as far as TV sports coverage was concerned.

So when the North Carolina basketball team went to Kansas City for the Final Four in 1957, the players were totally unaware that the games would be televised live in Carolina. C.D. Chesley, involved in local TV, had gone out to Kansas City to set up coverage.

"It was the first ACC basketball televised to the state," remembered Tar Heel broadcaster Woody Durham.

Two triple-overtime victories later, the Tar Heels were NCAA champions, flying high literally and figuratively. When their plane touched down at the Raleigh-Durham Airport, a shocking sight greeted them.

Some 10,000 cheering fans had turned out at the airport to greet their returning heroes, a surrealistic mob scene that stunned the Tar Heels. Pete Brennan knew that he and his teammates had done something special when they saw that crowd and when student friends started asking for their autographs.

The Tar Heels had indeed made an impact on their fans and their state. But it carried even further than that.

At the time, television hadn't made much of an impact on college basketball in the country, let alone North Carolina.

But after those thrilling North Carolina victories, interest in ACC basketball picked up all over the South. So did television coverage. Those two exciting victories over Michigan State and Kansas had inspired Chesley to start the ACC Saturday afternoon game of the week the very next season.

Fans who watch dozens of ACC games every week have C.D. Chesley to thank for his trail-blazing efforts.

CHAPTER SIX

The Sixties

I n a decade of social movement and dramatic transitions in America, things were also changing for North Carolina basketball.

Frank McGuire left in the wake of a gambling scandal and NCAA recruiting violations, and Dean Smith took over as the Tar Heels' head basketball coach in 1961.

Although the Tar Heels had finished No. 5 in the national polls and won the regular season ACC championship in the 1960-1961 season, McGuire called it "the worst year of my life."

For a couple of years it would not get any better for Smith. As time passed, however, a new golden era dawned at Carolina.

The "Underground Railroad" was dismantled; while Smith continued to recruit in New York, that wasn't the main focus of his widespread talent search.

Among the impressive new talents were Larry Miller, Bob Lewis, and Rusty Clark, who helped the Tar Heels win the ACC tournament championship in 1967 and gain a berth in the NCAA's Final Four, both for the first time in 10 years.

Then along came Charlie Scott as the Tar Heels made two more Final Four appearances. Smith had made a statement by recruiting Scott as the first black in ACC history, mirroring the social movement in America at that time. And Scott made his own statement at Chapel Hill by becoming one of the greatest players in Carolina history.

The Tar Heels had clearly turned the corner in the late sixties under Smith, posting an 81-15 record in the last three years of the decade.

The Rest Is History ...

Frank McGuire's program was being investigated by the NCAA for recruiting improprieties, and Smith, his capable assistant, was rumored to be moving to greener pastures.

"It will be only a matter of time before some school grabs him," a sportswriter said of Smith, who confirmed one report that he had turned down the assistant coaching job at Kansas, his alma mater. The year before, Smith was trying to land the head coaching position at Wyoming but just missed out.

Now he was playing it one year at a time at Carolina, hoping for the best.

"As far as I know right now, I'll be here next season," he said.

Smith could not know it at the time, but his life was about to change dramatically. The following season, McGuire was fired, and Smith became the head coach at Carolina.

And with the change, the face of North Carolina basketball would be changed forever.

A True Tar Heel

It was 1961 and a time of turmoil at Chapel Hill. The basketball program went on probation, and popular Frank McGuire left to coach in the NBA. Recruiting restrictions were imposed and the schedule cut sharply.

It wasn't exactly the most ideal situation in which to begin a head coaching career. So when Dean Smith was offered the job, McGuire tried to talk him out of it.

"Frank told me I shouldn't take it, starting out like that," Smith remembered. "Everett Case, who had gone through the same thing at North Carolina State, said we'd never recover from it."

McGuire asked Smith to join him as an assistant in the NBA, but Smith declined. "I didn't think I could cut it as a pro coach."

Smith dug in at Carolina, as befitted a Tar Heel. As expected, the first year was rough. The Tar Heels had an 8-9 season. Unexpectedly, they never had another losing season under Smith. And 36 years later, he retired as an institution at North Carolina.

Slow Start, Fast Finish

Dean Smith was a struggling young coach then, and his basketball future at North Carolina didn't look promising. After three years, his teams had a mediocre 35-27 cumulative record. He couldn't beat archrival Duke. Members of the student body were so unhappy with him that they had strung Smith up in effigy and set fire to the figure.

"In 1965, I did sit there and think, 'Maybe I'm not supposed to be doing this.'"

It is a good thing for North Carolina he didn't quit. Dean Smith went on to break the record for college basketball coaching victories. His final tally before retiring in 1997 after a 36-year career as a head coach: 879-254.

Smith actually turned his career around with a conscious decision.

"It was that I'm not going to live and die with each win or loss," he said.

Hanging in There

It was a late winter night in 1965, and a bus rumbled along the highway carrying the North Carolina basketball team back to campus. It had been a long ride home following a 22-point loss at Wake Forest.

Dean Smith stared out the window. He had a lot on his mind. The defeat had extended the Tar Heels' losing streak to four games, and their record was now an unremarkable 6-6. He was still trying to establish both himself and his team.

As the bus approached the Chapel Hill campus, a startling sight greeted Smith and his players. There, before their disbelieving eyes, was a crude figure of Smith strung up by a group of angry students. The effigy had been set on fire, and Smith was burning up in more ways than one. Finally, Billy Cunningham burst out of the bus to tear down the figure.

Smith's record would improve dramatically after the incident, starting with a victory only days later over archrival Duke. After that win, students asked Smith to talk at a pep rally.

"I can't," he said. "The rope's too tight around my neck."

Bob Lewis (left) and Billy Cunningham helped Dean Smith turn the basketball program around in the 1960s.

In Your Dreams

On a road trip with his North Carolina basketball team, Frank McGuire was sleeping in his hotel room when he was suddenly jarred awake by a sharp noise.

Standing at the foot of his bed in a trancelike state was Dean Smith, McGuire's assistant coach and road-trip roommate. According to McGuire, his sleepwalking roommate was crouched in a defensive stance as if playing a game.

"Once he shouted at me," McGuire once recalled. "I almost went through the ceiling."

Later when asked about the incident, Smith told a reporter, "I think Frank probably made that one up."

"But I guess I'm not really the one to ask," he added. "How would I know if I was asleep?"

Scrambled Message

One of the reasons for Dean Smith's success was his variety of complicated defensive formations. Louisville coach Denny Crum once compared Smith's switching defensive strategies to "a Chinese fire drill."

Asked to explain the strategies, one of the Louisville players told a reporter probably more than he wanted to know:

"Well, they've got the run-and-jump out of the straight man defense. Then they may go to a 2-3 zone, or a 1-3-1 zone. Or they'll use the run-and-jump out of the 2-3, or they'll trap you out of the 1-3-1.

"Sometimes, they'll pressure full-court man for man, or they'll run-and-jump out of the man for man. Or they'll go to what they call a scramble."

Got that, Mr. Reporter?

Misquoted

When he coached at Vanderbilt, Eddie Fogler wasn't on the best of terms with the press. He claimed that *The Tennessean* in Nashville misquoted him.

A former North Carolina point guard and assistant coach under Dean Smith, Fogler was once quoted as referring to his former mentor as "Dean."

Not so, said Fogler. Like all of Smith's players, including Michael Jordan, Fogler never called him anything but "Coach Smith."

To Eddie Fogler, it's still "Coach Smith."

Pointed Remark

Under Dean Smith, North Carolina players were taught to acknowledge good plays by teammates during a game. Particularly, the Tar Heels would point to each other after baskets.

One time against Maryland, it cost them.

After a victory over North Carolina, Maryland star Len Elmore was asked why it was so easy to score on the Tar Heels. "They were so busy pointing at each other after they scored," he said, "that we just threw the ball downcourt and scored."

Like Father, Like Son

He was a basketball coach who cared not only about his players, but about society in general. He believed in fairness, so he went against the general thinking and helped to integrate his team by bringing in black players.

If that sounds like Dean Smith, it should. But actually he wasn't the first in his family to break a color line. Long before Smith brought Charlie

Charlie Scott faced bigotry and a lot of pressure defenses.

Scott to North Carolina in 1966, his father was doing the same for black players in Emporia, Kansas. In 1934, Smith's dad had integrated the basketball team at Emporia High School.

"Dad got called on the carpet for that," Smith said. "He was told that Emporia would be dropped from the… conference. He persisted, because we were all taught to believe in the human family from day one."

Dean Smith's stand for integration at North Carolina was not only unpopular, but also more hazardous to his health than his notable smoking habit; his life was repeatedly threatened.

Smith was not afraid to take a stance on other controversial social issues during his time at North Carolina. He stood up against the death penalty in North Carolina, the Vietnam War, and the nuclear buildup.

"I wasn't trying to leave a legacy," he said. "I was trying to do what was right."

Sticking up for Scott

Dean Smith hated to lose. He hated intolerance more.

Once after a game at South Carolina, the Tar Heels were walking off the court when a fan called Charlie Scott a "big black baboon."

Two assistants had to restrain Smith from going into the stands after the fan.

"It was the first time I had ever seen Coach Smith visibly upset, and I was shocked," remembers Scott, the first black basketball player at North Carolina. "But more than anything, I was proud of him."

All in the Family

Anyone playing for Dean Smith was always considered "part of the family." It didn't matter if your name was Michael Jordan or Richard Vinroot.

Vinroot, Class of 1963, served in Vietnam in 1968. His most frequent correspondent was his mother. His second? Smith.

"He wrote to me weekly—'I hope you're doing well; keep your head down. . .'"

Smith's kindness extended to Vinroot's three children, all of whom attended North Carolina. According to Vinroot:

"Each one of them got a call from the basketball office during their first week at school, making sure they had tickets to the games. They said, 'Your dad played for Coach Smith; we want to make sure you're taken care of.' I don't know how he found out they were in school there, because I never told him."

What's in a Name?

His name is Charles Scott. Really.

"None of my close friends called me Charlie," he said. "Neither did my parents. It was like a stage name."

But to basketball fans far and wide, he was known as Charlie Scott when he played at North Carolina in the late 1960s and then in the NBA.

How did this happen? It started when Lefty Driesell tried recruiting him for Maryland. He called him "Charlie," and that name stuck in the media.

Southern Inhospitality

Just as Jackie Robinson had faced bigotry in breaking baseball's color line in 1947, Charlie Scott had his share as the first black basketball player at North Carolina in 1967.

"It was pretty bad," Scott remembered of the harassment he caught from fans during road games. "If our fans acted that way toward a visiting player, I would be ashamed."

The harassment didn't only come from the stands. Opposing players also were pretty inhospitable, "harassing me, talking to me, elbowing me, pushing me.

"Playing basketball was the easy part."

The Right Frequency

Imagine a time when no one wanted to broadcast North Carolina basketball games. It was 1961, and an unproven Dean Smith had taken over a beleaguered program following the dismissal of Frank McGuire. The only local sportscaster willing to work the games was Bill Currie.

By the time Smith turned the basketball program around, stations were coming out of the Carolina woods. Then everyone wanted to broadcast Tar Heel games.

"After Dean and his program became big, a radio station in Charlotte offered him $50,000 for the rights to do Carolina basketball," Currie remembered.

Smith declined the offer. He was going to stick with Currie's smaller station, even though it was only paying $10,000. After all, Currie had been with Smith in leaner days. And what was more important than loyalty and friendship?

When Currie moved to Pittsburgh in 1971, Smith kept in touch. One day he called Currie and learned Currie was preaching at a local church.

"The next week, he sent a $250 check to the church," Currie recalled.

Left-Handed Compliment

When Dean Smith was struggling in his early years at North Carolina, Lefty Driesell, coaching Davidson at the time, received a phone call from some Carolina alumni.

"We want to get rid of Dean," the alumni told Driesell. "We want you to coach."

Driesell wanted no part of it.

"I said to give Dean a chance. He made them eat those words."

Tired Signs

Dean Smith admittedly borrowed ideas from other coaches, most particularly Phog Allen at Kansas. Usually, he added his own wrinkles.

When Smith played for Allen in the 1950s, tired Jayhawks signaled when they wanted to take themselves out of games.

"But he'd forget about you once you were on the bench," Smith said of Allen. "So I let [North Carolina players] put themselves back in."

Something's Missing

It was the fall of 1961, and Dean Smith was all set for his first game as head coach at North Carolina. Everything had been worked out to the last detail, even the staff's seating arrangements on the Tar Heel bench.

Smith sat down, waiting for the game to start. It couldn't. No ball.

"I was so caught up thinking about so many different things that I didn't tell anyone to bring a ball out of the locker room," Smith recalled. "I had to send Elliott Murnick, our manager, back to get one."

Once the ball was brought out, the Tar Heels knew what to do with it. They beat Virginia 80-46.

Throwback

When Frank McGuire left a troubled North Carolina basketball program in 1961, there was a movement afoot from alumni to hire a big-name coach to replace him.

Little thought was given to a relatively obscure 30-year-old assistant coach by the name of Dean Smith. With the exception of William B. Aycock, then-chancellor at UNC-Chapel Hill.

It was his job to pick a successor to McGuire. In considering Smith, he remembered something that had happened in his own youth.

In 1937, Aycock was a newly hired history teacher at Greensboro Senior High School, now called Grimsley. Bob Jamieson, the Greensboro football coach, needed an assistant and asked Aycock if he would like the job. Aycock said he knew nothing of football. No matter. Jamieson offered to teach him.

"He taught me the plays with dominoes on the floor of his house," Aycock remembered many years later.

It was more than a lesson about football that Aycock learned with Jamieson, a high school coaching legend. He learned about how to build a winning team without cheating. Also how to deal with people.

Many years later, when it came time to pick a coach for North Carolina's basketball team, he chose Smith. His reason? Smith reminded him of Jamieson.

"Bob Jamieson was the precursor of Dean Smith as far as I was concerned," Aycock said.

Unconvincing Argument

When Dean Smith was offered the job as head basketball coach at North Carolina in 1961, he took it. But that was after he was positive he couldn't convince Frank McGuire to stay.

"Of course I wanted Frank to stay," Smith recalled. "I didn't know whether I really wanted it. I had an opportunity to go to Wyoming as head coach, and I thought that this was his place and where he should stay."

Smith and his wife, Pat, stayed up late one night with McGuire trying to talk him into remaining at Chapel Hill. McGuire had also received similar encouragement from Harry Gotkin, his New York friend who was one of the main contacts for his famed "Underground Railroad."

"We thought we had him sold on it," Smith said, "but then he left anyway."

Climbing a Mountain at the Hill

Times were tough for North Carolina basketball when Dean Smith took over as head coach in 1961. How tough?

The schedule was sharply reduced, along with the budget, and there was no participation in tournaments for the Tar Heels. North Carolina played only two nonconference games, against Indiana and Notre Dame.

Plus Smith could only recruit two players outside of the Atlantic Coast Conference area. "With [a reduced schedule], it's pretty hard to recruit," Smith said.

This was all the result of a reeling program placed on probation for illegal recruiting practices during Frank McGuire's time. There had also been a gambling scandal.

"North Carolina State's Everett Case had the same [problem]," Smith said, "so both programs were hurt by it. That gave Duke and Wake Forest a chance to come to the front at that time in history."

Despite the situation, there was good team spirit, as Smith remembered.

"I always believed basketball's a team game. I think our first year we had a great team. I mean, everybody gave it up to one another. We didn't have anybody that could really dunk the basketball, but I thought it was a fun team to watch."

The Tar Heels had an 8-9 record that season. It was the only time Smith would have a losing season in his 36 years of head coaching at North Carolina.

Feeling Blue

No matter how many hours of practice a basketball coach runs, sometimes the best ideas come to him during a game.

Playing against Georgia Tech one night, the Tar Heel starters looked "flat as pancakes," according to Dean Smith.

"I just said, heck, let's put in the hustle team, you know, the guys who were hustling in practice, and maybe it'll wake up these guys. I had seen it done by a high school coach in Pinkneyville, Illinois, a man named Dutcher Thomas. He used to play a second five throughout the second quarter and let them press.

"But anyway, I just threw those guys in, and they really got it going. They were stealing the ball and scoring. They almost caught up. When I put in my first group, they were great from then on."

This gave birth to one of Smith's concepts at North Carolina: the Blue Team, a group of second-stringers that played as a unit to give the starting five a rest and fire up the team when needed.

Crossed Signals

Everyone knew about the tired signal at North Carolina when Dean Smith was the coach: player on the court holds up a fist. It's a signal to the coach that he wants to be taken out of game to rest.

It was a policy instituted at the start by Smith due to his unforgiving style of basketball.

"When you're trying to press on defense and move without the ball on offense, no one could play 40 minutes," Smith said, "so I told them to take themselves out, and they'd tell me when to go back in."

This liberal policy was a result of Smith's experience playing for Phog Allen at Kansas. "My college coach would forget about you if you said you needed a break."

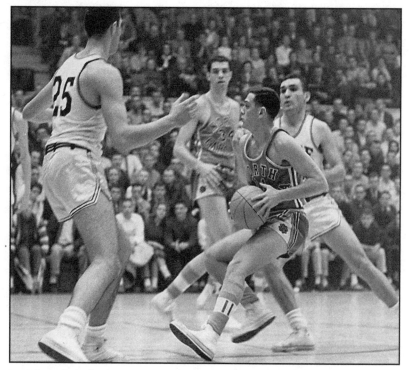

Larry Brown looks for the open man.

The first game that Smith coached at Carolina, it actually happened: Larry Brown and Donnie Walsh both gave him the tired signal, pumping their fists in the air.

Smith did nothing, exhorting them to "keep hustling." He thought the players were just showing spirit.

"I'd forgotten my own signal," Smith said.

Tiring Publicity

Dean Smith never imagined that the tired signal would hinder his efforts in bringing top players to Carolina. For a while it did.

"We got too much publicity [about the tired signal] in New York way back when," Smith said. "You know, guys would be giving the tired signal, and it would look like Grand Central Station."

As a rule, players took themselves out for no longer than 30 seconds just to catch their wind.

"It hurt us in recruiting for a while until somebody started realizing that our best players were still playing 37 minutes," Smith said.

A Good Walk Unspoiled

Charlie Scott, who broke the color line at Carolina, was well aware that the school was regarded as the liberal bastion among Southern universities. It was the main reason he wanted to play basketball at Chapel Hill. But first, he had to take a walk through town before making his final decision.

Dean Smith says Scott related this story to him:

"He took off by himself and walked into town. He wasn't with the coaches. Everyone was nice to him. He felt he belonged. He said he saw a couple hippies on Main Street, and then he really felt better."

A Weighty Decision

Basketball wasn't always Dean Smith's favorite sport.

"I liked football the best in high school because that gave me more leeway on the field," Smith recalled of his days as a high school quarterback in Kansas.

Smith also was a guard in basketball and a catcher in baseball. However, when he enrolled at the University of Kansas, he was told he had to choose between football and basketball.

Smith weighed only 155 pounds soaking wet. He selected basketball and didn't regret it, particularly after playing on the Jayhawks' 1952 national championship team.

Rusty Wasn't Rusty

If fans were to argue Dean Smith's most important player during his tenure at North Carolina, one name that probably wouldn't arise is Rusty Clark. However, a case could certainly be made.

During Smith's first five years as coach, a strong rebounding center was the one ingredient that the Tar Heels lacked. The six-foot-10 Clark supplied the muscle from 1966 to 1969 while playing on the first of Smith's great teams.

Clark was not the team's best player; that honor was held by forward Larry Miller. However, Clark was the final piece of the puzzle.

"Coach Smith always said that in order for the Tar Heels to be a really great team, they needed someone to bring up the ball and someone to rebound," pointed out Rick Brewer of the sports information office.

Clark took care of the latter as the Tar Heels won their first ACC title since 1957 and posted an 81-15 record during his time there. He was also integral in developing Smith's view of the Tar Heel blueprint for success.

Road Court Advantage

When Dean Smith first came to North Carolina in 1961, he believed it was important to play a strong nonconference schedule. He felt it helped the Tar Heels prepare for the tough Atlantic Coast Conference competition ahead.

Thus Smith made sure that schools like Indiana and Kentucky were generally on the schedule from year to year. There was only one problem with Kentucky: the Wildcats' coach, Adolph Rupp, refused to play any games on the North Carolina campus. His explanation was that Carmichael Auditorium did not have a big enough seating capacity.

Not that anyone north of Kentucky believed that was the main reason, but when any of the games were played in North Carolina, they were held either in Greensboro or Charlotte, but never at Chapel Hill.

When the situation was reversed, the games were more often than not played on the Wildcats' home court in Lexington.

Kentucky thus had a big home court advantage in the series. No matter. Smith's teams always had great success against the Wildcats, winning five of the first six games even though four of them were played on the Kentucky campus. The Tar Heels were also able to beat the Wildcats in Louisville.

North Carolina's success against one of the country's great basketball programs continued long after Rupp had left Kentucky. At one point, the Tar Heels won six straight games in the series. It wasn't until the 1990-

Larry Miller was always backed by his hometown fans.

1991 season that Kentucky finally played a game at Chapel Hill. It was part of a scheduled six-game series.

The game ended in controversy over who touched the ball last before it rolled out of bounds. The Tar Heels won 84-81, and Kentucky coach Rick Pitino was so angry that he had the rest of the series canceled.

The next time the teams met was in the NCAA playoffs four seasons later. Once again, Smith's team prevailed.

In 16 games with Kentucky, Smith's teams had a remarkable 13-3 record. It turned out that it didn't matter where the teams played; North Carolina always had the advantage over Kentucky.

Local Hero

When Larry Miller first came to North Carolina in the 1960s, he brought his own fans with him. More precisely, they followed him.

One day, 14 buses rolled into Chapel Hill for a freshman basketball game. They carried people from Miller's hometown of Catasauqua, Pennsylvania, a suburb of Allentown, who had come down to Carolina to watch Miller perform. Just about everyone from Catasauqua was there.

Before coming to Carolina, Miller had dominated just about every sport in Catasauqua and earned quite a reputation. So great, in fact, that when Miller started playing varsity ball at Carolina, the townspeople scraped up $4,000 to get Tar Heel games broadcast on an Allentown radio station.

It was money well spent, as far as they were concerned. For three years, Miller was the primary player on Dean Smith's early great teams in the late sixties. By then Miller's popularity had spread far beyond Catasauqua.

CHAPTER SEVEN

The Seventies

Season after season, Dean Smith had used the Four Corners offense, which frustrated opponents to no end, to perfection. It was also called the "Blue Plate Special," if you were listening to colorful Marquette coach Al McGuire, or "The Ford Corners," in reference to Phil Ford, the exquisite point guard who ran the exasperating time-wasting offense with the precision of a Swiss watch.

Not that the Tar Heels couldn't run and shoot with the best of them. In the NCAA's national semifinals in 1977, they had matched high-scoring UNLV shot for shot and beat the aptly named "Runnin' Rebels" 84-83 with a late rally.

Although the Tar Heels lost to McGuire's Marquette team in the finals, it did not overshadow the Tar Heels' success in the seventies.

Overall, it had been a solid decade for North Carolina basketball that included two trips to the Final Four, four ACC tournament championships, and an NIT championship.

The Tar Heels were ranked in the Top 20 all but one of the 10 years and boasted such fine players as Ford, Bob McAdoo, Bobby Jones, George Karl, Mike O'Koren, Dennis Wuycik, Walter Davis, Mitch Kupchak, Tommy LaGarde, and Bill Chamberlain.

Kick-Starting a Ford

Many basketball coaches will promise the world to a hot new recruit. But according to Phil Ford, Dean Smith did not.

He says Smith didn't promise a thing. In fact, he told Ford that he could very well start out with the junior varsity.

"That kind of set me back," says Ford. "But my mom really liked that, because she said, 'If he's not out here promising you that you will start, that means that if you go there and work hard and do the best that you can, then he won't be out there promising your job to another high school player.'"

Ford not only became one of the best practitioners of the Four Corners offense, but was named to the All-America team three times and was named the Player of the Year.

Coaching Phil Ford was a pleasure for Dean Smith.

Tar Heel Magic

Like Ford, George Karl was recruited by many college coaches and promised the moon by most of them. All except Dean Smith. Karl wasn't even sure he would start at North Carolina, but he was sold on the program as soon as he walked into the gym at Chapel Hill.

"They had a kind of no-nonsense, team-oriented 'we' mentality that I don't think any other coach had," Karl said. "There was a mystique to North Carolina that the other schools didn't have."

Mike O'Koren knew it was always pass first for Dean Smith's teams.

Bench Press

Mike O'Koren, who played for North Carolina in the 1970s, recalls how disciplined Dean Smith's teams were. Eight or 10 passes had to be made prior to taking a shot.

"We were playing Virginia during my freshman year," O'Koren remembered. "I got hot, I took a couple of shots, and then I took a bad shot.

"I came over to the bench, and Coach goes, 'That was a bad shot.' I said, 'But, Coach, I felt it.' He said, 'Oh. Go feel the bench.'"

Backing His Player

In his junior year, Mitch Kupchak had a back problem. The only solution was a difficult procedure, his spine had to be injected with an epidural block.

The operation was scheduled to take place on a Sunday morning after the Tar Heels arrived home from a Saturday night game at Clemson.

Waiting in the operating room, Kupchak was surprised to see Dean Smith suddenly walk in wearing a gown and a mask.

"I think he's pretty squeamish, but he was there, first thing on a Sunday morning," Kupchak remembered.

To say Kupchak appreciated it is an understatement.

"With my parents back in New York, it was comforting having him there with me," Kupchak said.

Miracle on Hardwood

The Four Corners offense, the foul-line huddle, and the clenched-fist tired signal were all familiar techniques of a Dean Smith team.

But it was something that a Smith team did not do that called just as much attention to itself. No timeouts were called unless they were absolutely necessary.

Smith didn't like calling timeouts early in the game because he felt he might need them at the end. Facing Duke one night in 1974, Smith was glad he had saved them.

The Tar Heels trailed the Blue Devils by eight points with just 17 seconds left in regulation.

Walter Davis's timely shots propelled UNC's "Duke Miracle."

Bobby Jones converted two free throws to cut Duke's lead to six. Walter Davis then intercepted a Duke pass and hit Jones for a layup. Duke's lead was now four.

Carolina then took a timeout.

When play resumed, Duke couldn't get the ball inbounds. North Carolina recovered, Davis hit a shot, and the Duke lead was down to two!

Duke inbounded the ball successfully this time, and North Carolina fouled. Pete Kramer went to the line and missed the shot. Ed Stahl got the rebound for North Carolina, and Smith called his last timeout to set up his most important play of the game.

When the Tar Heels put the ball in play, Mitch Kupchak threw a pass to Davis at midcourt, and the North Carolina forward banked in a 30-foot shot at the buzzer to tie the game.

The fans at Carmichael Auditorium were so excited they stormed the court.

Smith checked the scoreboard.

"My gosh, have we won or something? I thought the game was tied."

Then the fans went back to their seats and watched as the Tar Heels pulled out the game in overtime 96-92. Thanks to Smith's judicious use of timeouts, the legend of the "Duke Miracle" was born.

It Could Have Been Finer ...

Early in my career as a sportswriter for the Associated Press in New York, I took over the national college basketball beat. One of my main duties was to write the college basketball roundup. I wrote hundreds of them each season, always working hard not to duplicate a lead no matter how obvious the situation.

On my days off, there were capable staff writers who took over the roundup task, and each had his own unique perspective. One week I came back from my two days off to work the college basketball desk on a night mighty North Carolina was upset. It was the biggest basketball story of the night and the obvious top to the roundup.

Thoughtfully, I crafted my opening paragraph:

"Nothing could be finer than to beat North Carolina."

Clever, I thought. Unique, I thought. Brilliant, I thought. I went home that night satisfied I had written a sharp lead paragraph. Bring in the Pulitzer committee, please.

The next day in the office, I found a note of reprimand in my mailbox. It was from the assistant sports editor, and it was addressed to me and to the staff in general. It said in so many words:

"We've had enough 'nothing could be finer' leads on basketball roundups. Please, no more."

It seemed that North Carolina had been upset two days earlier when I was off. Guess what lead the writer had used to start the roundup?

Aw, Cut It out

"Are you the guy who cut Michael Jordan?"

Fred Lynch has answered the question many times, probably more than he would like. Lynch was one of the basketball coaches at Laney High School in Wilmington, North Carolina, when Jordan was trying to make the varsity as a sophomore in 1978.

It was decided then that Jordan would be better off playing his sophomore year on the junior varsity. Although Lynch readily admits to making the final decision to cut Jordan, it's a probability that other coaches were involved—namely one Clifton "Pop" Herring, who was the varsity coach then. No matter. Lynch continues to shoulder the responsibility.

"You can give all the explanations you want, but most people don't understand," Lynch said. "They look at him now and think he had to be tremendously good all of his life. He was good, but not fantastic."

In putting Jordan on the JV, Lynch inadvertently earned his own niche in North Carolina sports lore. He also provided Jordan with motivation.

"It was embarrassing, not making that team," Jordan said. "They posted the roster, and it was there a long, long time without my name on it. I remember being really mad.

"Whenever I was working out and got tired and figured I ought to stop, I'd close my eyes and see that list in the locker room without my name on it, and that usually got me going again."

Off by Miles

When Dean Smith was trying to recruit Michael Jordan for North Carolina, Lefty Driesell was trying just as hard to get him for Maryland. Perhaps a little too hard, as Smith remembers.

"We told [Jordan's] family that they could see Michael play a lot because it was close to his home," Smith said. "Lefty told Michael's family that Wilmington, [North Carolina,] was just as close to Maryland as it was to Chapel Hill.

"But Mr. Jordan said he had driven around the state and that wasn't exactly the case, that five hours wasn't the same as two."

Goodbye, Maryland. Hello, North Carolina.

Big Mac

Dean Smith didn't lose many recruiting battles for players that he really wanted. But when Tom McMillen slipped his grasp and went to Maryland, he had to do something he never did before.

Smith needed a big man, and so he went against his policy of recruiting a junior college player. Smith had a seniority system at North Carolina and was apprehensive that a JC player, already a junior, might create discord on his team.

No such problem. Bob McAdoo, a player that hardly anyone had heard of at Carolina, quickly fit in with the 1971-1972 team. He became an all-everything at North Carolina, including an All-American on the Associated Press team.

"Mac was the adopted child in the family," Smith said, "but it worked out beautifully."

Film Class

Dean Smith's passion for game films to critique his players was legendary at North Carolina. Along with the usual hard practice, Smith would sit with his team and watch the films, charting up to 23 different categories of player performance.

Although sometimes his players didn't always find it funny, Smith could. Once walking into the locker room for that day's session, Smith asked with a mischievous grin,

"What kind of practice today, boys, one- or two-reeler?"

Pranks for the Memories

The Wild Bunch was a popular movie of the time. North Carolina had its basketball equivalent with a collection of zany characters during the 1970-1971 season.

Nicknamed "The Wild Bunch" after the bullet-riddled western with William Holden, the Tar Heels that year were all about surprises, both on and off the court. No one expected them to shoot down a powerful South Carolina team, but they did. They also unexpectedly won the regular-season ACC title and later the NIT.

They all had colorful nicknames, including the "Cheetah," "The Gipper," and "The Zoomer." Perhaps the most important player was "Sophomore George" Karl. His fiery play inspired these Tar Heels to greater heights as they led the ACC in diving for loose balls, battling for rebounds and scraping for every inch of the court.

Along the way, this group also had a lot of laughs, mostly at each other's expense. It was a team that showed plenty of togetherness on the court and a lot of individuality off of it.

There was Steve Previs, who wrote plays and mimicked movie stars. He bore a resemblance to actor Jack Palance, a former Carolina athlete. There was Dennis Wuycik, who tossed around dead snakes in the dormitories.

"I thought it was a new necktie," Previs said after one landed on him. "I started to tie a knot in it but discovered it was a dead rattlesnake."

Lee Dedmon had a big appetite for both clothes and food.

"Lee has us all capped," Bill Chamberlain said. "He came in here with plaid pants, an Uncle Sam hat, a yellow double-breasted blazer, and two-tone shoes. There's no way to beat that."

One day at the training table, the cook announced that he had a surplus of steaks. Craig Corson set an all-time training table record by devouring five at one sitting—until Dedmon showed up. He polished off six.

From a basketball standpoint, it had to be one of Dean Smith's most satisfying teams. The season before, the Tar Heels had struggled to win 18 games in the final year of Tar Heel great Charlie Scott. Pessimism prevailed. How could North Carolina replace Scott? Somehow, the Tar Heels found a way with "The Wild Bunch." They won 26 games and a couple of championships.

"It's been fun to coach to win, instead of to keep from losing," Smith said at the end of the wild, wild ride of a season.

Blue Ribbon Special

Pick a season under Dean Smith, and there was usually some kind of nickname associated with the reserve unit. In 1972, it was "The Tall Blues."

According to Craig Corson, the tallest of the Blues, the nickname was related to a popular beer commercial of the day.

"We're always popping," he said, "like in Pabst Blue Ribbon tall blue cans."

Just Doggin' It

Dennis Wuycik acknowledged himself as the team mystic on the powerful 1972-1973 North Carolina squad. He could have been the team comic as well.

Once asked to name his favorite actress for the media guide, Wuycik responded, "The beautiful Pasha Bird."

Pasha Bird happened to be the name of his girlfriend's dog.

Chucking 'Em Up

Steve Previs, a key Tar Heel player of the 1970s, bore a striking resemblance to Jack Palance. And like the former North Carolina athlete turned actor, Previs was thinking seriously about a career on the stage and in movies.

Certainly his imitations of Dean Smith kept his teammates entertained. There was one Previs story about Smith's hard-driving practices that always had the Tar Heel players in stitches.

As the story went, Smith was conducting a particularly exhausting practice session one day, and Dennis Wuycik was on the line shooting fouls. Wuycik shot a free throw, Previs related, then vomited right there at the foul line. Then he shot another. Smith didn't blink.

"Nice concentration, Denny," Previs said, mimicking Smith's nasal Midwestern tone. "Manager, get a towel."

How About a Big Hand for the Big Fellow?

Tom McMillen's first appearance at North Carolina in a Maryland basketball uniform created quite a stir in Chapel Hill.

McMillen, a highly recruited Pennsylvania high school center, was not too popular at Chapel Hill after choosing Maryland over North Carolina in a last-minute reversal of field. Apparently McMillen was influenced by his parents, who preferred that he follow his brother Jay to Maryland.

Even before the basketball season started, McMillen was getting a lot of heat from the North Carolina fans. When North Carolina played a football game at Maryland, Tar Heel fans brought along a banner that said, "Say hi to Mom, Tom." The inference, of course, was that McMillen was a momma's boy.

Now the basketball season was here and Tar Heel fans were ready to boo him—or worse. North Carolina coach Dean Smith, who was disappointed at losing McMillen, thought it best to diffuse a potentially dangerous situation from the start.

Taking the arena microphone before the game, Smith told the fans to give McMillen a warm welcome. "He's a young man who wanted to come here to North Carolina," Smith said. "For various reasons, he did not, but he wanted to come here, and I don't think we should treat him badly at all."

Rick Brewer, North Carolina's sports information director, said it was the only time he had ever seen Smith do that.

By the time the North Carolina coach was through, the fans were ready to embrace McMillen, not lynch him. When they introduced the starting lineup and McMillen's name was called, he got a standing ovation.

"It was unbelievable how big that ovation was," Brewer recalled.

The crowd loved it even more when McMillen scored only two points and North Carolina won 92-72.

Comeback Kids

With so many great comebacks in North Carolina history, it is difficult to decide which is the greatest. High on almost everyone's list would be the Duke game of 1974, when the Tar Heels came back from an eight-point deficit with 17 seconds left to beat the Blue Devils in overtime.

But another North Carolina comeback against Wake Forest the following season wasn't too shabby, either. This happened in the ACC playoffs.

The Tar Heels trailed by eight points with about 50 seconds left.

"The game was hopelessly lost," recalled longtime sports information director Rick Brewer.

That's what most everyone thought. But North Carolina converted three turnovers into baskets in the last minute, including a misguided Wake Forest pass that nicked the scoreboard hanging over center court at the Greensboro Coliseum.

"Even the scoreboard was playing defense for the Tar Heels," remarked an observer.

North Carolina profited by a couple of missed foul shots by Wake Forest and then tied the score on Brad Hoffman's jumper with one second left in regulation. Then Phil Ford and John Kuester hit key free throws in the final seconds of overtime for a stunning 101-100 North Carolina victory.

Bugged

Talk about enthusiasm; Phil Ford had it in abundance. A player who could not sit or stand still for very long, the animated Ford was nicknamed "Bugs Bunny" for his emotional, team-stirring outbursts.

Amused by Ford's behavior, Dean Smith once remarked tongue in cheek, "People ask me why I play Phil so much. Well, his cheerleading and jumping get in the way on the bench."

Racing Ford

Sometimes Phil Ford's all-out effort put him in great danger, as well as endangering anyone sitting at courtside.

During one game against Georgia Tech, the irrepressible North Carolina guard twice chased basketballs clear over the end zone press tables. One time, he missed the sportswriters; another time he wiped one out.

Said one of the writers, "If Ford spends any more time out there, they're going to make him buy a ticket."

Perfecting the Shot

Any North Carolina fan worth his salt remembers the Duke game of 1974, but for Duke fans, remembering it would pour salt on the wounds.

The Tar Heels trailed the Blue Devils at Carmichael Auditorium by eight points with 17 seconds left. Miraculously, North Carolina managed to tie the game and then win in overtime.

Walter Davis made North Carolina's biggest shot, banking in a 30-foot shot at the buzzer to tie the game in regulation after a series of steals had helped the Tar Heels climb back into contention.

The year after Davis graduated, Smith brought him back to help with his coaching camp. Davis was in the gym talking to the kids when Smith walked in and pointed to a spot on the court.

"Now this is where Walter hit that shot that tied Duke in the '74 game," Smith said, then turned to Davis: "Walter, do you want to try it again?"

Smith tossed the ball to Davis, and he turned and shot from the exact location and with the same motion as he did in the Duke game. This time, the ball swished cleanly through the hoop.

"He didn't even hit the backboard," recalled longtime sports information director Rick Brewer. "But he made the shot again right in front of all these kids, which was absolutely amazing."

Did He Really Say That?

They were just six little words spoken on the air, but they came back to haunt Tar Heel sportscaster Woody Durham again and again, thanks to Dean Smith.

It was the opening round of the ACC tournament in Greensboro on March 6, 1975, North Carolina against Wake Forest. There were 50 seconds left when Skip Brown scored to give the Deacons a 90-82 lead. At which time, Durham said, "That should just about do it," sounding the death knell for Carolina.

Of course, after Durham had ruled out any hope for Carolina to make a comeback, the Tar Heels did just that. The Tar Heels beat the Deacons 101-100 in overtime.

"They were putting my radio audio on the game highlight film," Durham recalled, "and here I am, the Carolina announcer, saying that Wake Forest was going to win.

"Dean insisted that this be put on the highlight film. He used to joke all that year, and in the spring meetings, 'Now here's Woody, our own announcer, saying, "That should just about do it."' and he laughed about that."

Durham admits he should have known better, having seen Carolina wipe out an eight-point deficit in the final 17 seconds of regulation to beat Duke in overtime the year before.

Special Moment, Special Man

Severe vision problems that would have sidelined an average man did not prevent the extraordinary George Glamack from being one of Carolina's top scorers in the 1940s. It wasn't uncommon for "The Blind Bomber" to score 20 points a game in a time when teams were usually barely averaging 60. He was truly a Carolina treasure in his time.

But now it was 1979, and Glamack had acute arthritic problems that confined him to a wheelchair. He was living in Rochester, New York, and trying to get around as best he could.

When North Carolina traveled to Rochester for a tournament, Glamack received an invitation to be a special guest. Glamack was to toss up the ceremonial opening tipoff before the championship game.

As it turned out, Carolina was in the championship game against Niagara.

The Tar Heels were already in the warmup line when Dean Smith spotted Glamack sitting in his wheelchair at the edge of the court and walked over to greet him.

"Coach Smith talked to him for a second and turned back to the floor," remembered Carolina broadcaster Woody Durham. "I have never seen him do this before and never seen him do this since. He stopped the warmup drill, called the players over and individually introduced each of the players to George Glamack.

"I think it said a lot about what Glamack had meant to Carolina basketball."

It also said a lot about Dean Smith.

He Should Have Quit When He Was Ahead

Seeing is believing, but Woody Durham couldn't believe it when Walter Davis banked in a 30-footer at the buzzer to cap Carolina's incredible comeback against Duke in 1974. Probably the fans in Carmichael Auditorium couldn't believe it, either.

"When Walter released that shot, my first reaction mentally was, that's too strong," the Tar Heel broadcaster recalled.

It actually was. The ball hit the glass first before dropping through the basket to cap an eight-point rally in the final 17 seconds of regulation. Durham couldn't remember what he said when the shot went in. He had to wait until Dean Smith's television show later in the week to hear the sound from the game film.

"As it turned out, I said, 'Kupchak makes the pass to Davis, Walter turns, dribbles, lets fly, long shot…'"

At that point, the tape was silent.

"The crowd was quiet," Durham said. "It's interesting; on the audio tape you could hear the horn blow, because there's not much noise. And then suddenly, they just erupt. And then my comment was, 'UN-BE-LIEVABLE!' because I didn't think it was going in."

According to Durham, the next time that the team practiced, Smith told Davis to try the shot again. This time, he missed the basket and backboard completely.

Burned by the Freeze, But Just Once

Imagine North Carolina playing Duke and not scoring a single point in the first half. It actually happened on February 24, 1979, when the Tar Heels, playing in Durham, froze the ball from the opening tap. The idea was for the Tar Heels to hold the ball and let Duke come out and chase them, opening up possible back-door scoring opportunities. After all, it had worked for Clemson against Duke a couple of days earlier.

This time, the Blue Devils weren't biting. The half ended with Duke up 7-0, forcing Smith to open up the offense in the second half. The teams each scored 40 points after intermission as the game ended with Duke a 47-40 winner.

One week later, North Carolina faced Duke again, this time in the ACC championship game. This time, the Tar Heels didn't fool around and went right after Duke, ultimately claiming the victory 71-63.

"Coach Smith would never admit this, but I firmly believe he went to Durham to see if maybe he could beat Duke [with the slowdown offense], but setting the stage for a possible third meeting in the tournament a week later," recalled Tar Heel broadcaster Woody Durham. "He played them an entirely different way that night. I knew he would play differently than he would in Durham, because that didn't work, and so he took it to Duke."

True Blue

Like the pros, college players have groupies, too. In the seventies, one female fan wrote two or three letters a week to the North Carolina players—usually in Carolina blue ink.

"There's a rumor going around that Mitch Kupchak has gotten married and is living in a trailer camp," she wrote one time. "Could you please verify this rumor? Please let me know as soon as possible."

She had apparently run out of blue ink. She excused herself for writing in red, the North Carolina State color, ending her note with, "Boo Pack."

Another time, one wrote to the Carolina athletic department in the sixties:

"So sorry to see Dick Grubar get hurt on TV last Saturday. Could you please send me the towel he wrapped around his knee? If it has been washed, could you send me one he has touched recently?"

He Has a Point . . .

Although his basketball players had an unusually high graduation rate at North Carolina, Dean Smith wouldn't hesitate to advise one to leave early—if he was guaranteed to make big money in the pros.

Such a case was Bob McAdoo, a junior college transfer who stayed only one season at Carolina and joined the NBA in 1972. Explaining the situation at a news conference, Smith put it in language to which sports writers could relate:

"Look, if someone offered you a job with *Sports Illustrated* and you were a junior in college, wouldn't you quit?"

A 20-Game Winner, by George

George Karl, former Tar Heel star and a longtime NBA player and coach, was discussing Carolina's tribulations of the 2001-2002 season. The Tar Heels would not have a 20-win season for the first time in 32 years.

"The last time Carolina didn't win 20 games was my freshman year," Karl recalled.

That was the 1969-1970 season, the year that Charlie Scott was a senior. As a freshman, Karl was not allowed to play on the varsity that season.

The following year, Karl replaced Scott in the starting lineup, the only change to the starting five in 1970-1971. The Tar Heels improved from 18-9 to 26-6 and won an NIT championship. That started a string of 31 straight 20-win seasons.

Karl never teases Scott about it, though.

"Charlie kicked my butt so many times," Karl said.

They're Smokin'

When the Tar Heels played in the Rainbow Classic in Hawaii over the 1972 Christmas vacation, they brought along about 1,000 fans. There was no mistaking that they were from Tobacco Road.

"The thousand smoke more cigarettes in one night than 1,000 Hawaiians smoke in a year," noted one Hawaiian columnist. That included Tar Heel coach Dean Smith, a notoriously heavy smoker.

The Tar Heels were smoking, too, in another way. They knocked off Utah, Washington, and Louisville to win the tournament.

Crowd Control

As the 1972-1973 season unfolded, it became increasingly evident to North Carolina's cheerleaders that fans were getting harder to control. At many of the arenas that the Tar Heels visited, they were greeted by surly, hostile crowds and near-riot conditions. The cheerleaders decided to set a good example at North Carolina's next home game.

There was a jam-packed crowd at Carmichael Auditorium when Maryland came into Chapel Hill for a big ACC battle. As the buzzing crowd waited impatiently for the game to begin, the cheerleaders began unrolling a large paper banner on the sidelines.

The banner, featuring three-foot block letters, was 100 feet long. The cheerleaders paraded it around the court, and the message clearly set a pattern for that night's game. The sign read:

"We welcome Maryland as our guest. We only have one small request—lose."

The crowd remained reasonably sane, and the Terrapins held up their part of the bargain by losing. In relative peace and without the usual hostility so rampant in college basketball that season, the Tar Heels won 95-85.

Frank Who?

How times had changed. Frank McGuire was once a hero at North Carolina when he coached the Tar Heels to the national championship in 1957. But now in 1971, he was the enemy, coaching archrival South Carolina.

The Gamecocks expressed McGuire's chip-on-the-shoulder attitude with a punishing, physical style. Not only that, they were good—featuring such nationally recognized players as John Roche and Tom Riker.

The Gamecocks, ranked in the top 10, had rolled into Chapel Hill fresh from a triumph at the Holiday Festival in New York. It was an emotional moment, particularly with North Carolina's Dean Smith coaching against his old mentor.

If no one else thought so, Smith felt the Tar Heels could beat the Gamecocks. But they had to have a total team effort.

"I believe you can beat South Carolina, and I want you to believe it," Smith told his players before the game.

The message got through. In one of the shockers of the season, the Tar Heels managed to pull off a 79-64 upset that set Carmichael Auditorium rocking and rolling.

Around midnight, a couple of Tar Heel players were still sitting around the locker room, soaking in their great triumph as a caretaker cleaned up the place. The worker picked up a banner that had been piled on the floor.

"Hey, you guys want this thing?" he asked.

Dave Chadwick, a reserve who had come off the bench to play an important role against the Gamecocks, looked at the banner, which read, "Shoot the Birds."

"No," he said, "we don't want it. Give it to Frank McGuire."

How times had changed indeed.

Great Scott!

On February 25, 1970, the Tar Heels played a game that had more than the usual significance. It had nothing to do with national ranking, winning streaks, or records of any kind. It was Charlie Scott's last home game.

The contest was no match. The Tar Heels raced to an early lead and completely outplayed Virginia Tech.

With five minutes left and the Tar Heels totally in command, Dean Smith pulled Scott out of the game along with two other seniors, Eddie Fogler and Jim Delaney.

The crowd was on its feet, applauding. The noise in Carmichael Auditorium was deafening. And there was no letup in the applause. The crowd wanted more—they wanted to see their beloved Scott just one more time.

With a minute left, Smith relented. Back into the otherwise meaningless game went the Tar Heels' top scorer. The noise level went up another couple of notches, if that was possible.

Scott took a jumper from the side—no good. There was a collective sigh among the disappointed 9,000 fans.

Now Virginia Tech had the ball. No chance for the fans to see Scott score one last time, it seemed. But wait! Suddenly, there was a steal, a blue blur racing down court, a cross-court pass.

Scott was the blur taking the pass. Now he went up, up, up—and put the ball through the hoop. Bedlam! Everyone was happy.

Smith didn't ordinarily like to put starters back into a one-sided game that would embarrass the opposition. As it turned out, he had little choice this time.

Swan Dive

When George Karl played at North Carolina from 1969 to 1973, his physical all-out style thrilled Tar Heel fans. Never one to worry about scrapes and bruises, Karl was constantly diving for loose balls, earning the nickname "The Kamikaze Kid."

While Dean Smith loved to see his players drive hard and dive for loose balls, he thought Karl sometimes went overboard.

"George'd dive anytime," Smith said.

Almost History

George Karl was a political science major and normally a pretty good student at North Carolina, except for one course on ancient history, in which he showed little interest. Karl was pretty much in the dark about the class's subject, and the professor knew it.

This was Karl's final semester at Chapel Hill, and he had an opportunity to play basketball for a U.S. national team against the Soviet Union.

Could his professor let him take an early exam, so he could play for the U.S. team?

"Study the chapters on the Peloponnesian War," said the professor, a big Tar Heel basketball fan.

Karl insisted he didn't know anything about the Peloponnesian War.

"Study them," the professor insisted.

Karl knew he ought to do some reading; otherwise he wouldn't be graduating with his class. When he took the early exam, there was only one question on it:

"Who won the Peloponnesian War?"

Karl marked down "Sparta."

George Karl goes to the hoop against Maryland.

It was the correct answer, and Karl was free to travel with the U.S. team and graduate on time.

On the Dean's List

Karl played for Dean Smith from 1969 to 1973. Many years into his own coaching career in the NBA, Karl was still getting pointers from Smith.

"I still get letters from Coach Smith," Karl said in 2001. "He's taken some clippings and circled the number of times I've used the word *I*. 'Don't we mean *we*, George?' I judge my year on how many times I hear from him on that."

Well, He Was in a Sling. . .

Tickets for the ACC basketball tournament are always hard, if not impossible, to get the day of a game. It was never more the case than in 1975, when North Carolina played North Carolina State. The Tar Heels featured the great Phil Ford, and the Wolfpack, the great David Thompson.

As early as dawn, fans were patrolling the streets of Greensboro looking for tickets. One creative type held up a sign that read, "I'm not a picket. I need a ticket."

He wasn't nearly as creative, though, as one particular fan who walked around with his arm wrapped in a sling, playing on the sympathy of others. Naturally, someone took pity on him and sold him a ticket.

How surprised do you think the seller would have been to see that same person at the game applauding and cheering wildly? Of course, the sling was gone.

Sticking to It

What's a Tar Heel, anyway?

Trivial pursuers may want to know this. Also anyone fascinated by nicknames attached to college teams or just interested in American history.

Here's the scoop, according to one story:

During the Civil War, North Carolinians were among the fiercest fighters against the North. They put up stiff resistance, literally digging in their heels against the enemy.

In one of the battles on the outskirts of Petersburg, Virginia, in 1864, Robert E. Lee reportedly said, "There they stand as if they have tar on their heels."

As the first university in the state, the nickname naturally became North Carolina's team name.

CHAPTER EIGHT

The Eighties

S maller was better as the eighties featured the electronic revolution and the flow of free markets around the world. Computers with their tiny chips had indeed made the world a smaller place.

Not so in college basketball. By then, bigger seemed to be better. TV was starting to make its impact on sports in a big way, and the NCAA was continually moving major events into larger arenas.

Like the Super Bowl, the Final Four grew into a national event worthy of a big stage. In 1982, the NCAA held the Final Four at the New Orleans Superdome, where professional and college football games were usually played. The place was jammed with 61,612 fans.

It was big. In fact, the purists asserted that it was too big for a college basketball game. Somehow the game between North Carolina and Georgetown matched the grandeur of the stage. Like many North Carolina games that year, this one came down to the final minute.

And when Michael Jordan hit the pressure go-ahead shot in the final minute and Carolina held on to win, it relieved a lot of the pressure on Dean Smith. Six times before, including 1981, he had brought a Tar Heel team to the Final Four and come back each time without the NCAA's biggest prize.

Curses, Foiled Again

Thoughts of the day: offensive boards, defensive balance, and hands up on defense.

"Yeah, I still remember that," says Michael Jordan of the daily grind of practices under Dean Smith.

There was something else that Jordan remembered of his days at North Carolina: The Tar Heels' coach allowed no cursing.

"You had to run the steps if you cursed," Jordan says. "I had to run the steps a couple of times."

About Par for the Course

Dean Smith was always known as a pretty good motivator. It wasn't only basketball that inspired some of his best pep talks. Ask Roy Williams, Smith's longtime golfing partner.

One day on the course, the two were paired against Bob Knight and a congressman from Illinois. They were tied going into the ninth hole when Smith hit a shot off the tee that sailed out of bounds.

Knight and his partner were in great shape. They were both on the green looking at probable two-putt pars. Williams, meanwhile, had an almost impossible shot above the green to get up and down to halve the hole.

As Williams thought about his shot, Smith walked over for a chat.

"By the time Coach got through pumping me up," Williams recalls, "you'd have thought Watson and Nicklaus would have come to me to ask how to play the shot."

The pep talk would have made Knute Rockne proud. Williams's putt would have satisfied Watson and Nicklaus. Of course, Williams made par.

Stacked Against Him

Bob Staak always had the greatest respect for Dean Smith's coaching ability. Sometimes too much respect.

Recalled the former Wake Forest coach, "One game that we won, we're up three with two seconds left. We had the ball—and I was concerned something's going to happen."

The Same as Night and Day

Bill Guthridge was Dean's Smith's top assistant for 30 years and a perfect complement to North Carolina's head coach. Both worked long hours, rarely taking a day off during the basketball season. Describing their lifestyles one day, Guthridge quipped, "He's a night person. I'm a morning person. So we pretty well have the clock covered."

Wait a Minute …

As a coach, Dean Smith stressed team over individual. Ask Michael Jordan, the least hyped two-time Player of the Year in college basketball history.

When he was head coach, Smith abolished box score stat sheets in the locker room.

"You [usually] have the highest point total at the top, and that doesn't do it for me," Smith said.

When a North Carolina player did get a chance to look at a stat sheet, it was prepared the Smith way—alphabetized and the number of minutes played eliminated.

Reaching Too High

It was the 1982-1983 season, and like so many games against North Carolina, time was running out for Maryland. Chuck Driesell, son of Terps coach Lefty Driesell, had a chance to score the winning layup. But the shot was blocked by Michael Jordan, as he had blocked many a shot in his Carolina career.

"I know a man has confidence in his son," said Tar Heel coach Dean Smith, "but I didn't know that much."

Nobody's Perfect …

Bruce Ogilvie has made quite a reputation for himself as a sports psychological pioneer. There was at least one time in his career, though, that his evaluation missed the mark.

Ogilvie examined Michael Jordan when he was a freshman at North Carolina. Afterward, he got Dean Smith's ear.

"I told him, 'This young man is well put together. He really sees the big picture.' Then I remember telling Dean Smith, 'I just hope he can play basketball.'"

Not over His Head

Michael Jordan wasn't always as supremely confident as he is today. When he first committed to North Carolina, he wasn't quite sure if he could compete with all of the great athletes at Chapel Hill.

But he found the answer quickly enough during a campus pickup game prior to the Tar Heels' first practice. On the court were people like Mitch Kupchak, Al Wood, and James Worthy, all great Tar Heel talents.

"Al Wood was guarding me, and it was tied; next basket wins," Jordan recalled. "I had the ball. I was nervous because people were watching and I wasn't sure I belonged out there.

"I went baseline, and he went with me. When I made my move, [seven-foot] Geff Crompton came over to help out. I went up with the ball and thought I was trapped."

But Jordan just kept going up and dunked over both players.

"When I came back down to the floor, I said to myself, 'Was that really me?'"

Great Expectations

Like any college freshman, Michael Jordan faced some uncertainty upon entering North Carolina. This was intensified by the expectations of him as a basketball player.

"I thought I would go in and be a flop," Jordan says. "Everyone was expecting so much."

But Dean Smith gave Jordan some advice that helped him not only at North Carolina, but in future years.

"He said to treat it like something you really enjoy and not to treat it like a job," Jordan remembered.

Throwing away Money

Michael Jordan lives for competition. It doesn't matter if it's a basketball game… or a Monopoly game.

Once at North Carolina, he and roommate Buzz Peterson and their dates were playing Monopoly. When it was obvious Jordan would lose, he tossed what was left of his money at Peterson and stormed out of the room.

"I stayed with my sister that night," Jordan remembers, "I just couldn't face Buzz."

Michael Jordan: "Everyone was expecting so much."

Pressure Player

With a game on the line, Michael Jordan always wanted the ball in his hands. It didn't matter whether it was a pickup game or for the NCAA championship.

With time running out at the NCAA Finals in New Orleans in 1982, Jordan hit the winning shot for North Carolina, a seven-footer with 17 seconds left. At Carolina, it is now known simply as "The Shot."

"He told me he knew that he was going to take that last shot to win it," says golfer Davis Love, a fellow student at North Carolina at the time. "Knew it. Dreamed about it. Most of all, he wanted it. He wanted the ball in that situation. How many freshmen would have that confidence to take it, then make it?"

Courting Jordan

At North Carolina, Michael Jordan could usually be found on a basketball court. If not there, Jordan often could be located on the golf course.

There, Jordan's golfing companions were usually Davis Love, a fellow student who would eventually join the pro tour, and Jordan's roommate Buzz Peterson.

If Jordan or Peterson were hard to reach, Dean Smith usually knew where they would be.

"Eventually, Dean got hold of me and told me to get those guys off the golf course and back on the court," Love remembered.

Not the Most Likely

Michael Jordan was not always the go-to guy on a basketball court. His childhood in North Carolina was spent waiting hours to play in pickup games.

"When you're young [and] pick your friends, you always want to pick the most popular guy," Jordan says. "I was never one of those guys."

Later, when Jordan committed to North Carolina, friends told him he would never succeed in basketball.

"Everybody thought I made a dumb move going to a Division I school," Jordan recalls. "They thought I'd sit on the bench for four years, come home, and work at the local gas station."

But Jordan thought differently.

"I took it in my mind that I had the opportunity to go to a Division I school and I was going to make the best of it," Jordan said.

Dean Smith told Jordan: Work hard, and you'll get the opportunity to play.

"I worked hard," Jordan said.

Camping out

When Michael Jordan was a high school senior, he didn't get much attention outside of Wilmington, North Carolina. Certainly not like Buzz Peterson, the High School Player of the Year in North Carolina who eventually became Jordan's roommate at Chapel Hill.

One college coach did notice Jordan, however. He was Roy Williams, Dean Smith's assistant. Williams suggested that Jordan be invited to the Five-Star basketball camp in Pittsburgh, where high school players compete and show off their talents to college coaches.

Not for the first week, however. That was reserved for the top prospects, and it was feared Jordan might be overmatched.

When Jordan showed up in the second week, he simply captured the spotlight.

"He just steps on the court and he's like playing a different game," remembered Tom Konchalski, a high school evaluator at the prestigious camp.

P.S.: Jordan won Most Valuable Player honors the week he played.

Campus Comfort

It's called "The Wall," and Michael Jordan remembers it very well. The brick fence that circles the library on the Chapel Hill campus was a popular meeting place for the most prominent athletes of North Carolina.

"When I was a freshman coming in, when I was being recruited," Jordan recalled, "I came up there on a Friday and there were the names sitting on The Wall: Kelvin Bryant, Lawrence Taylor, Al Wood, James Worthy, Sam Perkins.

"All these guys just sitting on The Wall, relaxing, joking, and picking at each other. When they come back and walk on campus, they sit right there on that wall."

After Jordan made a name for himself, he would often come back and visit the campus, making a stop at The Wall, naturally.

"It's very comfortable," Jordan says.

His Number's up

Famous athletes are usually associated with their numbers. Every sports fan knows that No. 3 belonged to Babe Ruth, No. 4 to Lou Gehrig, and No. 5 to Joe DiMaggio.

Michael Jordan is one of those rare superstars associated with two, and there's a family story involved.

Michael grew up worshipping his older brother Larry. Michael was in grade school when he played one on one with his brother in the backyard, where their father had set up a court.

"Back then, Larry was a little taller and much stronger," James Jordan once remembered. "Larry would beat Michael unmercifully. As Michael got older, he got bigger, and the games became much closer."

When Larry Jordan played for Laney High School in Wilmington, North Carolina, he wore No. 45. When Michael joined the team, he wanted to pay tribute to his brother. Of course, he couldn't wear the same number. He picked No. 23 because it was about half of his brother's number.

Jordan wore No. 23 at North Carolina and with the Chicago Bulls until he retired the first time. When he came out of retirement, Jordan switched to No. 45.

Slight Miscalculation

Michael Jordan had things pretty well figured out in high school. Only thing was, he figured wrong. One year he took a home economics course. His reason?

"I wanted to learn how to cook and clean and sew and all that. I figured no girl would ever want to marry me, and I didn't know if I'd have enough money to eat out."

Picture Perfect

The basketball game had long been over. The young fan, wearing Michael Jordan merchandise practically from head to toe, had been waiting patiently for his hero to appear. His father and a friend stood by his side.

Finally, Jordan came out of the players' entrance.

Would Michael pose for a photo, please? No problem.

Jordan put his arm around the young fan, as if they had been old pals. The youngster beamed.

The father prepared to take the picture. But something was wrong; the camera wasn't working. Frustrated, he tried a couple more times. Then the friend tried it. Nothing.

Finally, a man appeared carrying his own camera. He looked at the malfunctioning camera for a few minutes. Then, snap. The young fan was thrilled. He now had visual proof that he had actually met Michael Jordan.

The process had taken much longer than anyone could imagine, nearly five minutes. But Jordan, no doubt exhausted after a night on the court, had patiently waited until the boy had his photograph.

Putting the Bite on

Think of Michael Jordan and probably the first thing that comes to mind is "Air Jordan," his ability to seemingly fly to the basket. Also, that trademark of sticking out his tongue during these creative flights of fancy.

Jordan says he learned that tongue-wagging style from his father, James Jordan. His father had a habit of sticking out his tongue while at work.

At North Carolina, Jordan's tongue-wagging style created some concern.

"We told him Coach Smith wouldn't like him running around with his tongue hanging out," said Sam Perkins. "I told him, 'You're going to bite on it one day.' And, sure enough, one day he did. We all said, 'We told you so.'"

Dress Rehearsal

It was 1989. Dean Smith figured it was about time to change the look of the North Carolina basketball uniforms, particularly the outdated bellbottom warmups. So he called Alexander Julian, a noted fashion designer who grew up in Chapel Hill, graduated with the Class of 1969, and devotedly cheered on the Tar Heels. Julian was up to the job.

"Having Dean Smith ask you to redo the Carolina uniforms," Julian said, "is like having God ask you to redo the uniforms for the archangels."

Before the new uniforms were donned for the 1991-1992 season, Julian asked for advice from no less than Michael Jordan. Julian figured Jordan knew something about fashion, considering his face had been on the front pages of such magazines as *Esquire* and *Gentlemen's Quarterly*.

Smith gave Julian only one restriction: Keep the V-neck, "because it's unique to Carolina." Otherwise, he gave him free reign. Julian was experienced. After all, he had introduced teal to the NBA while designing the Charlotte Hornets uniform.

The redesigned Carolina playing uniform was pretty much the same as it had been, as it turned out. But, oh, those warmups! Stretch denim jackets with a new shade of Carolina blue. And pleated shorts, with argyle side panels on both shorts and shirts.

"It's a great outfit to take on a date," quipped senior Hubert Davis.

Trimmed

A word from Dean Smith could praise a player to the skies or cut him down to size.

When Sam Perkins was late returning from a haircut in Durham just a few miles away, he missed the team meal. The North Carolina coach was angry.

"We have barbers in Chapel Hill, too," Smith snapped.

A Stock Tip

When Michael Jordan left North Carolina for the pros, he told roommate Buzz Peterson he was having a shoe named after him.

"I said, 'Come on, no way,'" Peterson remembered. "He said, 'Yeah, they are. You better buy Nike stock.'

"I told him, 'You're a good player, but you're not going to go into the NBA and tear it up.'

"He said, 'OK, but you better buy Nike stock.' I should have listened to him. I could have made a penny or two."

"Peanut" Jordan?

What famous basketball player was nicknamed "Peanut" in high school? None other than Michael Jordan.

"Mike was real skinny, and we called him 'Peanut' because of the way his head was shaped," remembered Kevin Edwards of Jordan at Laney High School in Wilmington, North Carolina. "But I remember putting my hand up against his—we were both five-foot-nine—and his was twice as big as mine. We knew he wasn't going to stay five-foot-nine for long."

The Long and Short of It

Michael Jordan is one of the players who started the trend of wearing long, baggy shorts in the NBA. It was nothing new for Jordan. He had started wearing them at North Carolina.

Jordan "always liked his shorts bigger," recalled Bill Guthridge, Dean Smith's longtime assistant coach. "Michael just wanted them to fit loose."

Brad Daugherty's first day was unforgettable.

At Chapel Hill, the players could order any size shorts they wanted. According to Guthridge, Jordan always ordered his one size larger.

Memorable Day

Brad Daugherty's first day at North Carolina was one he will never forget—and for good reason.

"They had someone carry my bags to my room, and Coach Smith said, 'This is the last time anyone will carry your bags. From now on, you'll be like everyone else. We all carry our own bags. We do things for ourselves.'"

The North Carolina basketball coach constantly reinforced the lesson of self-discipline throughout Daugherty's college career. That included going to class, one of Smith's highest priorities for his athletes.

Smith wasn't kidding, as Daugherty remembers.

"If you cut a class, the next morning you ran with [assistant coach] Bill Guthridge at 6 a.m. You had to run four and a half miles with Coach Guthridge, and he's an avid runner. If you lost, you never heard the end of it at practice that afternoon."

Slamming Sam

Sam Perkins was one of the greatest players ever to wear Carolina blue. A six-foot-nine forward/center, Perkins's long arms and great reach allowed him to play much taller. He finished his four-year Tar Heel career in 1984 as the school's leading rebounder.

Usually low key, Perkins stayed out of controversy–except for one comment that created outrage in the state of Georgia and might very well have cost the Tar Heels a berth in the Final Four.

North Carolina was scheduled to meet the Georgia Bulldogs in the 1983 NCAA East Regional finals. When reporters asked Perkins for his observations about the Bulldogs, he said he had none. He should have stopped there. But he went on to say that he had no idea where the school was located or in which conference the Bulldogs played. Nor did he care.

The Peach State, and particularly the Bulldogs, took umbrage to Perkins's abrupt dismissal of the team. It was bulletin board material, all right. The inspired Bulldogs went out and upset Carolina despite another solid game from Perkins of 14 points and 11 rebounds.

When the next season began, Perkins was singing a different tune. Talking to the media, he said he had taken some time over the summer to

Sam Perkins was in the middle of many of UNC's big 1980s wins.

brush up on the conference affiliations and school locales of all North Carolina opponents.

A Higher Authority

An NCAA title in 1982 took a lot of pressure off Dean Smith, although North Carolina's student newspaper took the occasion to poke a little fun at the Tar Heels' celebrated coach.

Headlined *The Daily Tar Heel*: "And on the Seventh Try, Dean Smith Created National Champions."

A Hairy Situation

Dean Smith didn't allow his players to wear beards—at least not until James Worthy told him that he had a skin problem and couldn't shave close.

"OK," Smith said, "if you get a doctor's note, I'll let you wear one."

Worthy did and played his Carolina career with a well-manicured beard. The only time that Smith asked him to shave was for a *Sports Illustrated* cover in 1981 with Smith, Jimmy Black, Matt Doherty, and Sam Perkins.

One Degree of Separation

With players like Michael Jordan, James Worthy, and Sam Perkins, Chris Brust's name does not usually come up when fans talk about North Carolina's 1982 national champions.

But when a fan finds out that the relatively unknown Brust was indeed a part of that famous team, the inevitable question comes up. What was it like to play with Jordan?

Hero worship being what it is, just knowing someone who knows someone who is famous can be a thrill to some people. So of course, Brust is never far away from Jordan questions. The story he likes to tell the most:

"This person walks up to me and says, 'Do you know Michael Jordan?' I said, 'Yes.' He said, 'Could you write down on a piece of paper that you know him?'"

Brust jotted down the note, and the fan walked away satisfied that he had been close to greatness. Just one person away, that's all.

Taking a Dive

Name a sport and it seems that Michael Jordan has tried it. He might think twice about joining a swimming team, though.

Once in Wichita, Kansas, for a high school all-star game, Jordan was involved in a game of pool tag at his hotel. One of the players tagged Jordan especially hard. Jordan wasn't going to let him get away with it.

Jordan went after the player with a vengeance. Realizing that Jordan was not going to give up, the pursued player jumped into the deep end of the pool and remained underwater.

That didn't stop Jordan. Into the pool he went, although he was never that strong of a swimmer.

"He swam more like a rock than a fish," remembered Buzz Peterson, Jordan's roommate at North Carolina.

Jordan sank to the bottom. Peterson had to dive in to help Jordan swim to the side of the pool.

"This remains one of the only times I can remember Michael being embarrassed due to his athletic performance," Peterson says.

Air Doherty?

While announcing his second retirement from basketball in 1999, Michael Jordan listed his game-winning shot against Georgetown in the 1982 NCAA finals as one of the two greatest of his career. The other was the shot he made to beat Utah in the 1998 NBA Finals.

Unlike the Utah game, Jordan, only a freshman, was not the first option against Georgetown. North Carolina coach Dean Smith said the idea was to get the ball inside to either James Worthy or Sam Perkins. Jordan was to take the shot only if either of those players wasn't open.

Here's what happened:

With 32 seconds left and the Tar Heels trailing Georgetown 62-61, Smith called a timeout to design the play.

Time back in. UNC point guard Jimmy Black, with the ball, looks inside. Nothing. He passes over to Matt Doherty at the free throw line. Doherty passes it right back.

Black goes to his right and fakes a pass to the closely guarded Perkins. Georgetown's attention is drawn away from Jordan, wide open at the left-side wing.

Black fires the ball to Jordan, who calmly sinks a seven-footer with 17 seconds left.

North Carolina 63, Georgetown 62!

"He didn't have a hesitation or a doubt that he was going to shoot the ball," remembers Doherty. "He took that shot like it was in pregame warmups.

"When he got the ball, I was open at the free throw line, and I joked that if he had passed me the ball, I would have knocked down the shot and everybody would have been talking about Air Doherty, not Air Jordan. Of course, we know that's not true."

A Worthy Player

And you think that North Carolina's one-point victory over Georgetown in the 1982 NCAA Finals was the only close call the Tar Heels had in the playoffs that year? Everyone remembers that thrilling 63-62 victory over the Hoyas, but few recall that the Tar Heels were almost upset by James Madison University in the second round of the East Regionals.

"We almost took James Madison for granted," James Worthy recalls of JMU, which was ranked No. 9 to North Carolina's No. 1. "We didn't pay much attention to the tendencies of that ballclub."

Worthy came to the rescue, however. He scored North Carolina's last five points, including two free throws after drawing a charge on Charles Fisher in the final minute. The free throws put North Carolina ahead for good 52-46, and the Tar Heels held on to win 52-50.

"They deserved to win," Worthy said of JMU, "because they had us."

A Worthy Superstition

When the Tar Heels won their regional NCAA tournament in 1982, it was James Worthy's turn to cut down the net. He would have nothing of it.

The year before, Worthy had participated in the traditional net-cutting ceremony in the regionals before North Carolina lost to Indiana in the Finals.

"I didn't want to jinx myself by participating too early," Worthy said. He told everybody, "I'll cut 'em down in New Orleans."

That's where the Tar Heels were headed to play in the Final Four. Two victories later, Worthy and his teammates fulfilled that promise, of course.

James Worthy reached for greatness at Carolina.

No. 1 in America,
No. 2 in North Carolina

It was 1983, and North Carolina State had just won the NCAA championship. But although the Wolfpack were national champions, coach Jim Valvano still knew his humble place in the state of North Carolina.

"This'll really be big news back home," Valvano said, "unless Dean Smith retires tomorrow."

Hey, It's Still Carolina

Shortly before the 1987-1988 season, the North Carolina Tar Heels received the bad news that J.R. Reid and Steve Bucknell were involved in a bar fight in Raleigh. Dean Smith suspended them for the opening game.

It didn't matter to Smith that the opener happened to be in the Tip Off Classic against Syracuse, the nation's No. 1-ranked team. Discipline was discipline.

Then more bad news: Kevin Madden, another starter, got caught in a slow elevator on game day and was late for the team bus. Smith's policy: If you're not on time, the bus doesn't wait. It doesn't matter who you are, so the bus left without Madden.

By the time he got to the arena on his own, Madden learned he wouldn't be starting. Again, discipline was discipline.

In a rare circumstance, Smith started three freshmen. Somehow, it didn't matter. Even with two of their top players out of the lineup and another one not starting, Carolina was Carolina, and the Tar Heels beat the Orangemen 96-93.

A Ford and a Jet

The greatest point guard in Tar Heel history? For Dean Smith, it was Phil Ford without question. But could Kenny Smith be far behind?

Ford launched the point guard tradition at North Carolina when he came to Chapel Hill in 1974. Kenny Smith, among others, carried it on with style. He was named National Player of the Year by the *Basketball Times* in 1987.

To be sure, there were other great Tar Heel point guards through the years. To name a few: Jimmy Black, Jeff Lebo, King Rice, Derrick Phelps, Jeff McInnis, and Ed Cota.

You could make a point for Smith—actually 768 of them. That's how many assists Smith chalked up in his career from 1983 to 1987. The total broke Ford's school record but was in turn broken by Cota in 2000.

Like Ford, Kenny Smith not only directed the offense but scored plenty of points himself.

"Just because you're a point guard doesn't mean you can't score," Dean Smith said. "You just want points; it doesn't really matter where they come from."

Dean Smith was one of the first coaches to use the term *point guard*. It referred to the player at the point of attack, the one who brought the ball upcourt and directed the offense. Dean Smith thought it would be a good idea to develop a primary ball handler, rather than split the responsibility between the team's two guards.

Kenny Smith, a native of Queens, New York, was nicknamed the "Jet" because of his exceptional quickness and speed. Once assessing the great North Carolina guard, New Jersey Nets scout Al Menendez said, "He's a greyhound. Not a shepherd, not a pit bull—a greyhound."

Learning a Lesson

Like all the other Tar Heels who played for Dean Smith, Michael Jordan learned that teamwork was more important than individual accomplishment.

This was particularly impressed upon Jordan after one game against Maryland. In the final minutes, Jordan had stolen the ball, raced down the court, and scored on a spectacular dunk to win the game for North Carolina.

No matter. As the deliriously happy Tar Heels charged into the dressing room, Dean Smith caught up with Jordan and pointedly told him, "You know, Kenny Smith was wide open!"

Oops, Our Mistake

When Ranzino Smith arrived at North Carolina in 1984, nobody in the basketball department rolled out the blue carpet for him. Same for Hubert Davis in 1988.

Smith was a five-foot-11 guard who had played at Chapel Hill High School. Davis was a frontcourt player who had played in Dean Smith's camp, but who, like Ranzino, was not a highly regarded college prospect.

Sure, they would get their scholarships at Carolina but never really play much. Why not go somewhere where they could play full time? That was the suggestion from the Carolina coaching staff.

The Tar Heel staff usually wasn't wrong in sizing up players. This time was different.

"Smith wasn't supposed to be here but became an important player for us," remembered Rick Brewer, the longtime Carolina sports information director. "He was an incredible threat, a dynamic shooter."

Smith wound up playing 128 games in Carolina Blue, and as a senior, he made about 41 percent of his three-point shots and averaged 11.7 points a game.

After Smith left, Davis became one of the top threats in the North Carolina offense. He played in 137 games and starred as a senior in 1991-1992, averaging 21.4 points a game. Later, he became one of the NBA's leading three-point shooters.

For two guys that the Tar Heels didn't want, Smith and Davis did all right for themselves at Carolina.

Tell It Like It Isn't

It was the 1988 NCAA playoffs, and Dean Smith didn't sound happy. Even though the University of North Carolina was hosting early-round games, the Tar Heels were not permitted to play at home under new NCAA rules.

Instead, they were forced to fly a couple thousand miles out to Salt Lake City to play in the West Regional. And now they had to face Loyola Marymount, a high-powered scoring machine averaging more than 100 points a game.

Smith peddled his doubts to the media: How would the Tar Heels keep up with this team that played an NBA-style game?

Meanwhile, back at Chapel Hill, Duke had no such complaints. The Blue Devils were heavily favored over North Texas State and well rested to boot. They only had to make an eight-mile trip from Durham to Chapel Hill to play in the early-round games. Ironically, the Blue Devils were playing on the home court of the team their fans loved to hate.

Because Carolina was one of the host teams for the first two rounds, sports information director Rick Brewer stayed back to handle media relations. Of course, Brewer also kept an eye on the Carolina game when he could.

J.R. Reid was a big factor in the 1988 NCAA playoffs against UNLV.

"I walked back to the interview room, and there were a couple of TVs there," he said.

This is what Brewer saw: the Tar Heels shooting three-pointers like crazy and getting the ball inside to J.R. Reid. In short, playing an NBA-style game. North Carolina simply outscored the nation's highest scoring team 123-97.

Just about that time, Duke had also finished off North Texas State by a big score, as expected. Duke coach Mike Krzyzewski walked into the interview room with one of his players, Billy King.

"What's the score [of the Carolina game]?" Coach K asked Brewer.

"North Carolina won 123-97."

Then, Coach K turned to his player.

"What did I tell you on the bus ride over?"

"You said they would blow them out," King responded.

Apparently Smith had no one fooled by his pregame rhetoric, certainly not one of his greatest rivals.

Have a Minute, Coach?

The day after a game, it was Dean Smith's practice to grade the film as to how each player did. This usually took two or three hours, and he didn't want to be disturbed.

Rick Brewer, who worked with Smith longer than any other sports information director at North Carolina, knew that this was a sacred time for Smith and his staff. Brewer went to great lengths to make sure that the coach wasn't bothered. Sometimes, he had no choice.

"I think someone had died. Maybe Clair Bee," Brewer recalled. "Something dramatic had happened, and newspapers wanted a quote.

"The secretary was scared to death. In fact, that day they warned me. I said, 'I've got to do this. I've got to interrupt him. I've got to ask him one question.'"

Brewer got his quote but says it was the only time that he ever disturbed Smith during his film-grading sessions in more than 25 years.

One Game at a Time... Really

Many coaches love the cliché, "One game at a time." For Dean Smith, it was literally the truth.

Whenever Smith would walk into his office following a game, he would find two videotapes and a scouting report on his desk that he could take home to study.

One of the videos was a tape of that night's game. The other was a tape of the Tar Heels' upcoming opponent, with a scouting report on that team as well.

"That's the first time he would see a scouting report on the team they were playing next," said Rick Brewer, Carolina's longtime sports information director.

"People used to joke that he doesn't mean one game at a time, that he must be looking ahead. But that was the truth. He did not pay that much attention to any game but the one he was playing."

Projecting Themselves

Can you picture Michael Jordan carrying around a heavy film projector on North Carolina's road trips? No joke. Same was true for Phil Ford.

It didn't matter that they were on their way to stardom. They were also freshmen.

That was the rule on a Dean Smith team—freshmen carry the projectors so the coaching staff could study the films and prepare for the upcoming opponent.

Like good soldiers, the freshmen did their part—although the division of labor changed dramatically from year to year. For instance, when Jordan played, there were only two freshmen to split the projector carrying duties. Jordan took one handle, while Buzz Peterson claimed the other. When Tommy Lagarde played at Carolina, there were five freshmen to share the load.

The advent of VCRs changed the situation, of course.

"It was a big break for them," noted Rick Brewer. "They didn't have to worry about carrying the projectors around anymore."

On the Road Again

Under Dean Smith, the Tar Heels were truly road warriors. Name a place, big or small, and it's likely the Tar Heels traveled long distances to play there.

It mostly had to do with Smith's promise to recruits that the Tar Heels would play in their home area at least once so that their families could see them in person.

Thus, one year the Tar Heels played at UCLA and Pepperdine because of Scott Williams, who was from California. Another time they played in both Houston and U-T Chattanooga because Matt Wenstrom was from Texas and Jimmy Braddock was from Tennessee.

Smith also made frequent visits to New York to play in Madison Square Garden as well as New Jersey to play in the Meadowlands. Such players as Kenny Smith, Matt Doherty, and Mitch Kupchak were from the New York area.

There was another reason that Smith liked to play in New York: publicity. He felt it was important to showcase North Carolina to fans, writers, and potential prospects in the big town.

Be Like Michael?

What's in a name? For sports stars, it means a lot in terms of recognition. Try Shaq, for example. Or Tiger, the Babe... or Michael.

Actually, Michael Jordan was called "Mike" by some of his teammates when he was a freshman at North Carolina. In fact, that's how he was listed in the basketball media guide.

Sports information director Rick Brewer had second thoughts, though.

"Half the players would call him Mike; someone would call him Michael," Brewer recalled. "I wanted to get it straight."

One day Brewer wandered into the North Carolina locker room and found Jordan in there all alone, lacing up his sneakers for practice.

"I walked over and said, 'Look, half these guys call you Mike, half these guys call you Michael; how do you want us to refer to you in the media guide?'

"He said, 'I don't care, it doesn't make any difference to me, whatever you want.' I said that Michael has a better ring to it. Michael sounds a little better. He said, 'That's fine with me.'"

It was also fine with Dean Smith, who referred to all of his players by their proper names. And soon Michael Jordan became, well, Michael Jordan. Of course it was always Michael, except for one particularly memorable marketing campaign. You know, "Be Like Mike."

Burned out

For as long as anyone at North Carolina could remember, Dean Smith had a notorious smoking habit. In fact, it was a two-pack-a-day habit.

For some time, he had talked of quitting. Then came the start of the 1988-1989 season, and he decided that enough was enough. But how to quit? Smith had the perfect time and place.

On the first day of practice, all the beat writers, columnists, and TV people that covered the Tar Heels arrived to do their preseason stories. First, they talked to the players; then they interviewed Smith.

The large group of reporters assembled in the stands at the Dean Smith Center to talk to Smith. He answered every question about the team patiently and thoroughly but also casually added a bit of news about himself.

When he dropped the news that he had stopped smoking, it was like dropping a bombshell.

"Of course, that was the lead story in the papers the next day; forget about what the players said," sports information director Rick Brewer recalled. "This was a big deal. This guy's been a two-pack smoker all his life.

"But he was smart because of the way he did it. He did it publicly so he put the pressure on himself. He knew everyone was going to be watching."

According to Brewer, Smith has never had a cigarette since.

Don't Blame Dean

It turns out that Dean Smith, with his team-oriented style, wasn't the only one that could hold Michael Jordan under 20 points. Add the NCAA to the list.

During Jordan's sophomore season at North Carolina, the Atlantic Coast Conference was experimenting with the three-point shot. Jordan averaged exactly 20 points that season in the ACC.

But when the NCAA released its statistics for the 1982-1983 season, Jordan's average was just under 20. The NCAA still did not recognize the three-pointer in its records.

No Sleeping in Class

Dean Smith was intent on having his basketball players graduate and went to great lengths to make sure they did.

For many of the Tar Heels' away games, they would fly on chartered planes so that they could get back the next morning for class.

Assistant coach Bill Guthridge would remind the players, "Go to class. Eight o'clock class. Be in class sitting in the front row. It will impress your professor. He saw you play last night until 11:15 and you're here in his class."

Occasionally one or two of the assistants would wander around and make sure the players were in class. The chartered plane would also help on the other end of the trip.

"If we were playing, say, at Clemson at 9 o'clock on a TV game, we probably wouldn't leave here until noon to fly out, because you'd want them to go to their morning classes," said Rick Brewer. "Most teams would go in a day earlier so they could rest."

Self-Improvement

No wonder Michael Jordan's a winner. Just one story from his days at North Carolina emphasizes the obvious.

After each season, Dean Smith would call every player into his office and tell him what he needed to work on to improve his game. Smith told Jordan that he needed to improve his defense.

Jordan worked on that aspect of his game all summer. When he came back, in his very first game as a sophomore, Jordan's off-season work had paid off. When the Carolina coaches graded the game film, they recognized Jordan as the defensive player of the game.

"Knowing how competitive he was," remembered Tar Heel broadcaster Woody Durham, "that was a highlight for him."

Michael's One-Man Show

At the height of his professional career, Michael Jordan made a habit of taking over games. It should come as no surprise that he also did the same at North Carolina, as early as his sophomore year.

One of those occasions happened February 10, 1983, when North Carolina battled Virginia and All-America center Ralph Sampson.

The Tar Heels trailed Virginia by 16 points with about nine minutes left, then by 10 with 4:12 remaining.

Suddenly, Jimmy Braddock hit a three-pointer and Matt Doherty converted both ends of a one-and-one.

The deficit now stood at five.

Sam Perkins had another one-and-one opportunity and sank both shots to cut Virginia's lead to 63-60 with 2:54 remaining.

Perkins was forced to foul Sampson. The Virginia star went to the line in a one-and-one situation with 1:20 left and missed the front end.

Enter Jordan.

Braddock missed a three-point attempt for Carolina, but Jordan was there to slam in the rebound.

Then, as Randy Carlisle brought the ball upcourt for Virginia, Jordan stole it, went in, and scored to give the Tar Heels a 64-63 lead.

Carlisle missed a potential game-winning shot for Virginia, and guess who was there to grab the clinching rebound? Jordan, of course.

"I thought James Worthy was a better college player [in that era]," said Tar Heel broadcaster Woody Durham, "but you go back and look at the tape at some of the things Michael did. He was the most competitive."

A First-Class Operation

Does North Carolina treat its basketball players any differently than other schools? On at least one occasion, the Marquette basketball team found this to be true.

It so happened that both teams were on the same flight one day from Chicago to Dayton. The plane was stalled on the runway at O'Hare Airport for about two hours because of a rainstorm.

When the plane finally got to Dayton, the teams were forced to share the court for practice. A Chicago writer asked one of the Marquette players if he had a chance to talk to any of the Carolina players while they sitting on the plane.

"No, not really;" the Marquette player replied, "most of the Carolina players were sitting in first class."

Dean of Coaches

More than one coach in the ACC had a tough time going up against a Dean Smith team. Facing Smith's image was sometimes even tougher.

The late Jim Valvano liked to tell the story about the time he took over the basketball program at North Carolina State.

"My first week as coach at State, I went to the barber," Valvano said. "I sat down, and the barber says to me, 'So you're the new coach at State. You took Norm [Sloan's] place.'

"I introduced myself and he says, 'Well, I hope you have better luck than old Norm did.'

"I say, 'Didn't Norm win a national championship?'

"And he says, 'Yeah, but he was no Dean Smith.'

"I say, 'Dean Smith is certainly a great coach, but didn't Sloan go 57-1 at one point?'

"And he says, 'You're right. But just think what Dean Smith could have done with that team.'"

The Bald Truth

It seemed everyone at North Carolina wanted an arena named after Dean Smith except the man himself. In fact, Smith was hesitant to talk about the honor with reporters.

"It's never been a goal of mine to have a street, an arena, or a bathroom named after me," Smith said before the first basketball game at the Dean Edwards Smith Center on January 18, 1986.

The more questions he got about the new arena nicknamed the "Dean Dome," the less he wanted to talk about it.

"I don't like the word *Smith*," he said jokingly. "Dean Dome? No, that's worse. It makes me sound like I'm bald."

Smith enjoyed his postgame press conference much better. Then, he could talk about North Carolina's momentous 95-92 victory over Duke in a battle of the nation's No. 1 (North Carolina) and No. 3 (Duke) teams.

Cashing in

It was in the middle the 1985-1986 season, and North Carolina looked like it was about to lose its first game of the year. The Tar Heels trailed Marquette by nine points with 3:44 left.

But they rallied and finally tied the score at 64 with 36 seconds left. Then, trying "to make something happen," North Carolina's Kenny Smith drove the lane and was fouled.

Standing at the line with a hostile Marquette crowd trying to unnerve him, Smith suddenly felt something hit his cheek. It was a penny, tossed by a Marquette fan.

Smith didn't miss a beat. He calmly converted two shots for a 66-64 Carolina win that kept the Tar Heels' unbeaten streak alive at 19.

After the game, Smith said he didn't pay any mind to the Marquette fans, who also threw toilet paper when he was standing at the foul line.

"I hope next time they throw dollar bills," he said. "That will get my attention."

Win One for the Quipper

Dean Smith's longtime dominance in the ACC infuriated many a coaching opponent. One day after the ACC meetings, Maryland's Lefty Driesell herded all of the other coaches into a private room.

"Listen, we have to get together and do something about Dean," Driesell told the other six coaches. "I'm tired of him whipping us all the time."

Jim Valvano, a brash, wisecracking young coach from New York, was new to the league at North Carolina State. Never known for his lack of sarcasm, Valvano quipped, "Tell you what, Lefty, when you play him, I'll send my best guys over. When I play him, you send yours. This way, maybe, we'll have a chance."

Just a Matter of Time

Leave it to Dean Smith to put a positive spin on an 18-point loss.

His Tar Heels received a whipping from Arizona 70-52 in the 1988 NCAA's West Regional finals, which sent the Wildcats to the Final Four. With time differences the way they were, the Tar Heels were the last team to lose a regional final. That had to count for something, Smith reasoned.

"Well, we reached the Final Five," he quipped.

Double Talk

Dean Smith had more than his share of success against Lefty Driesell's Maryland teams, particularly at Cole Field House. However, Driesell could boast of at least one special achievement: His team handed North Carolina its first loss at the Dean Smith Center when it opened in 1986.

Driesell's name and that particular game came up many years later when Smith was chatting with reporters at the annual North Carolina media day before the start of a season.

Smith was reminded of how Maryland turned the game around with the help of Len Bias, who stole the ball from Steve Hale and scored in the final minute of regulation.

"It's funny you bring that up," Smith said. "I was looking at that game on film this summer and you know what? Bias double-dribbled on that steal."

One reporter raised an eyebrow.

"Dean, Len Bias is dead. Can't you let him rest in peace?"

Smith fixed a stern look on the reporter.

"Lots of dead men have double-dribbled," he said.

Smith's Spiel

At the start of the 1989 Maui Invitational in Hawaii, North Carolina, with seven players on their way to the NBA, was a heavy favorite over James Madison. Not as far as Dean Smith was concerned, however.

At the pretournament banquet, all Smith could talk about was the talent on his opponent's team and how lucky North Carolina would be to win.

Lefty Driesell, the James Madison coach, had dealt with Smith for many years while at Maryland. He had heard his shtick before.

Soon it was Driesell's turn to talk. Grabbing the microphone, Driesell smiled.

"Dean Smith's the only man in the history of basketball who's won 700 games and been the underdog in every one of them," he said.

No Excuses for Jimmy V

When he was at North Carolina State in the 1980s, Jim Valvano had as much trouble as any coach in the ACC against North Carolina, maybe more. Some ACC coaches were of the opinion that Dean Smith was an intimidating factor for young officials, worth at least a couple of points to his team.

Valvano disagreed.

"My experience in the games we've played against Carolina has not been a problem with the referees," he said. "Our problems have been with the guys in the blue shirts [North Carolina], not the striped shirts."

Dicey

Buzz Peterson, Michael Jordan's roommate at North Carolina, remembers that Jordan could be "pretty cocky."

"He'd be the type to say, 'I'll beat you in cards, pool, ping-pong, football, anything.' And everybody would say, 'Oh, shut up, we're tired of hearing your mouth.'"

One day Jordan's competitive nature really got him into trouble. Jordan was winning in a card game when one of the players asked if he could play dice. Sure, Jordan said, even though he had no idea how to play.

"He couldn't say no," Peterson remembered, "and they took total advantage of him. Everything legal. They killed him and spent all his money before he even found out. He wanted nothing more than to learn how to play, come back, and take their money. He was so mad."

Piling up

Talk about a paper chase; Dean Smith never threw away anything. He saved all 36 years' worth of practice plans in one place or another. Many of them were on his desk or spilling over from cardboard boxes in his big walnut-paneled office. Trying to find them at a moment's notice was sometimes tougher than solving the Tar Heels' baffling defenses.

"I'm extremely organized in practice," he said one day, "but that's the only place."

Noted Linda Woods, the director of basketball operations when Smith was coaching, "He deals in piles, not files."

When It Rains, It Driesells

In this corner, Dean Smith of North Carolina… and in this corner, Lefty Driesell of Maryland. No joke. This was sometimes one of the more contentious coaching relationships in the Atlantic Coast Conference.

At one point, Driesell sent an angry letter to Smith, informing the North Carolina coach he would refuse to shake hands after their games. When they next met, Driesell's discourteous reception sparked a near free-for-all between the Carolina and Terrapin coaching staffs.

When Driesell finally decided to make contact with Smith after games, he didn't exactly extend the olive branch. Running past Smith on the court after one game, Driesell slapped the North Carolina coach behind the head. It had to hurt.

"I was just giving him a low-five," Driesell said.

CHAPTER NINE

The Nineties

I t was hard to tell which was the biggest story of the nineties: the collapse of the Soviet Union, the fear of heightened terrorism, or the amazing run of the bull market on the New York Stock Exchange.

But at North Carolina, the biggest story was clear. It was the retirement of Dean Smith, who was calling it a career after 36 years as head basketball coach at Chapel Hill. Well, to call it just a career would be doing Smith a disservice.

Few coaches have impacted a university, or a sport in general, as did Smith. It had as much to do with the high graduation rate of his athletes, his sense of social justice, and his loyalty to friends as it did with his record 879 victories, numerous championships, and innovations. When Smith departed, he left a university in mourning.

After Smith made his announcement in October 1997, a sign outside of Sutton's Drug Store in downtown Chapel Hill implored: "DEAN, OLD FRIEND, PLEASE SAY IT AIN'T SO."

A chapter had been closed in North Carolina basketball history, but not before Smith added another NCAA championship title in 1993 and four more visits to the Final Four that brought his total to 11.

No one thought it unusual when the Tar Heels advanced to the Final Four two times in Bill Guthridge's three years as coach. Business as usual at North Carolina. That optimism didn't fade, even after a losing season under Matt Doherty in his second year—Carolina's first since 1962.

Like the stock market, it was a terrific run for the Tar Heels with six visits to the Final Four from 1991 to 2000. It would only be a matter of time before they would turn things around. As sure as the sky is Carolina Blue.

The Tar Heel Stamp

Look at NBA history and you'll find North Carolina well represented. What makes a Tar Heel player so attractive to NBA teams?

Jerry West says the typical North Carolina athlete is usually "very disciplined, personally a super kid, and a player who is very familiar with a winning program and also dedicated to win."

That apparently holds true for front office people as well. When West left his general manager's position with the Lakers in August 2000, he was replaced by a former North Carolina player, Mitch Kupchak.

Talk About Big...

Why couldn't he win the big one? Dean Smith used to hear it all of the time, critics continuing to emphasize his relative lack of success in the NCAA's championship round.

At a Final Four one year, Smith faced the all-too-familiar question. By then he had been to the Final Four eight times and had come home with the NCCA title only once.

When a reporter asked Smith about not winning his share of "big ones," à la John Wooden, who had won 10, Smith had had enough.

"The big one?" he said. "To me, the big one was the gold medal. You talk about big…"

Smith was referring to the U.S. Olympic team that he coached to a gold medal victory in 1976 at Montreal.

Smith would answer his critics at the 1993 Final Four with a victory over Michigan. That gave him his second NCAA title to accompany that Olympic gold medal.

Driving Mr. Thompson

Like many others, Georgetown coach John Thompson flew to Chapel Hill to honor Dean Smith when he announced his retirement

Dean Smith always had his finger on the pulse of a game.

prior to the 1997-1998 season. As expected, it was a frenzied day for Smith, full of interviews, phone calls, and a plethora of well-wishers.

Late in the day, Thompson needed a lift to the airport. Guess who drove him? Smith, of course. It was so typical. While the whole basketball world was heaping its praise on Smith, all he wanted to do was drive a friend to the airport.

Bad Timing

It was the 1992-1993 season, and the Tar Heels were going through late-game situations at practice. Donald Williams was trapped and called a timeout to avoid turning the ball over.

Dean Smith stopped practice. "No one uses a timeout unless I tell them."

Later that season, the same situation came up for Michigan in the NCAA's championship game, and the Wolverines wasted a timeout. That would cost them, when at the end of the game Chris Webber called a timeout his team didn't have. Michigan was forced to turn the ball over to North Carolina, and Smith had his second NCAA title.

"After it was over, I remembered what Coach Smith had said," said George Lynch.

Politically Incorrect

Senator Dean Smith? Smith actually considered running for that office at one time. That was before he had a talk with his wife.

"Some time ago a friend wanted me to run for the Senate [against Jesse Helms], and I said, you know, I wouldn't mind it," Smith remembers. "My wife said, 'Wait, Dean, you hate cocktail parties and making speeches. Why would you want to do that?' She was right."

Picky, Picky...

Few basketball rivalries equal the North Carolina-Duke clash. It was especially intense when Dean Smith was coaching against Mike Krzyzewski, when both teams were usually in the top 10.

It hit the heights (or, depending on how you look at it, the depths) when a sign appeared in the Duke stands that said, "J.R. Can't Read." In chiding North Carolina's J.R. Reid, the elitist Duke students had gone over the limit as far as Smith was concerned.

Smith was furious. He did some research and found that the combined college board scores of two of his players, Reid and Scott Williams, were actually higher than two of Duke's top players, Danny Ferry and Christian Laettner. He let everyone know about it, too.

To say the relationship between Smith and Krzyzewski cooled at that point was an understatement.

Precursor

Dean Smith was walking across campus one day when he ran into Tar Heel wrestling coach Bill Lam.

"How ya doin', Coach?" Lam asked Smith.

"I'm really tired," Smith said.

Despite the negative response, Lam remained cheerful and upbeat.

"Oh, when you hit the floor the first day of practice, you'll get that shot of adrenaline and be ready to go," Lam said.

"I'm really tired," Smith said again.

Lam didn't know what to make of such negativity from Smith. But he should have known something was up. A couple of days later, the 66-year-old Smith announced his retirement.

Change of Seasons

Bill Guthridge always knew never to trust April. It was usually in April, after another long season, that Dean Smith said he felt like quitting.

"After the season, we'd get him out to play golf, getting him to relax," Guthridge said. "And I always knew that if late August rolled around and he said, 'I'm sick of playing golf,' we had him."

When the fall of 1997 rolled around, Smith still wasn't quite ready to quit golf. At that point, Guthridge had a clue that Smith would retire, which he did.

Nearly Lionized

Now coaching for Penn State, Bill Guthridge? Yes, the longtime loyal assistant to Dean Smith once actually said yes to the Nittany Lions.

This was in 1978, after Guthridge had stood faithfully by Smith's side for 11 years. He had his plane ticket to State College all ready. The Nittany Lions were going to introduce him as their new coach.

Following a legend wasn't so tough for Bill Guthridge.

One day before Guthridge was scheduled to leave for his press conference, North Carolina had lost to San Francisco in the NCAA playoffs. Watching a tearful Phil Ford undressing in the locker room, Guthridge had second thoughts about the Penn State job.

Boarding his plane the next day, he only checked his bags as far as Chicago. From the airport, Guthridge called Smith to tell him that he was staying at North Carolina after all.

P.S.: When Guthridge replaced Smith as the Tar Heels' head coach in 1997, he didn't have to interview for the job.

Me Coach, You Player

Bill Guthridge usually played the bad cop opposite Dean Smith's good cop. He took care of discipline because, according to assistant coach Dave Hanners, "Coach Smith was so compassionate."

"Coach Gut," as he was called by players, also had his lighter moments. Guthridge usually took part in good-luck handshakes and often displayed a droll wit with the players. Any of them who would query "Coach?" might hear Guthridge respond, "Player?"

A Nice Ring to It

When Bill Guthridge replaced Dean Smith as head basketball coach, he figured his cell phone would be a standard part of his coaching equipment.

"As his assistant I could make just about every decision I wanted to," Guthridge said. "And if I didn't want to make one, I could say, 'Better go see Dean.' So this year, if you see me get out my little portable phone with two minutes to go in a game, you'll know who I'm calling."

No Overtime for Dean

Dean Smith could never bring himself to announce his retirement in advance or have a one-season "victory tour" before leaving his coaching position at North Carolina.

"Can you imagine how many rocking chairs I'd get?" the 66-year-old Smith said at the time of his abrupt retirement announcement before the 1997-1998 season.

A Drop in the Bucket

It was the 1993 NCAA playoffs, and North Carolina was tied with Cincinnati late in the game. There were eight-tenths of a second left in regulation, plenty of time to win as far as Dean Smith was concerned.

Gathering his players around him during a timeout, he set up just exactly how the play would go. The idea was to get Brian Reese open in the lane, where he could score an easy layup.

Just before the Tar Heels broke the huddle, Smith emphasized, "Now, Brian, you won't have time to dunk the ball; just drop it in the basket and we'll win."

Everything went as planned—except for one little thing. With a close-in shot, Reese decided to dunk, and the ball rattled off the rim. No goal. Overtime.

"We were like, 'Brian, Coach did everything else for you. Why didn't you just drop it in?'" Pat Sullivan remembered.

Reese was spared the goat horns. The Tar Heels won in overtime and eventually secured Smith's second national title.

Sign of the Times

There were TV trucks, rental vans, and even a couple of catering vehicles jamming the parking lot, all there for one of the biggest events in North Carolina sports history: Dean Smith's retirement.

Only one empty space remained in the lot, marked: RESERVED AT ALL TIMES. It was Smith's.

There was also space for sentiment. Someone had scribbled in chalk, "We love you, Dean, please don't leave."

All Greek to Them

Pay attention, now. You're in Basketball/Philosophy 101, Professor Dean Smith presiding.

Smith often relied on Greek philosophers to structure his own coaching philosophy. Once before a big game, he wrote this quote from first-century philosopher Epictetus on the practice plan, "Make the best of what is in your power. Take the rest as it happens."

The Tar Heels did, walking off with the NCAA title in 1993.

Message in a Locker

Dean Smith was known for giving his practices a theme, usually a succinct little saying that you might find in a Chinese fortune cookie. Smith would regularly stop practice to ask a freshman to repeat the thought of the day.

These thoughts were almost always generic. On one occasion, Brian Reese found the saying on a practice schedule put in his locker and knew it was personal.

Reese had been a star at a New York high school and came to Chapel Hill in the early 1990s with a reputation as an aggressive, defiant player. Reese would dunk on an opponent and then glower at him, shouting "On you!"

The saying that Reese found in his locker:

"A Tiger Never Roars After A Kill."

Making the White Team Blue

The date was January 5, 1995. It was a practice day, and the Tar Heels wandered into the locker room, checking out the day's schedule. As usual, it was the White Team (regulars) vs. the Blue Team (reserves), but something puzzled the players.

Penciled in to play guard on the reserve team was "Jordan."

"I thought Coach was just trying to make a point," said Charlie McNairy, one of the Blue Team members. Maybe Dean Smith was trying to send a message that one of the reserves was trying to act like a superstar.

But when the players actually saw Michael Jordan in shorts and sneakers, their mouths dropped open. Jordan was planning to announce his return to the NBA following his brief retirement to pursue baseball, and he needed some court action.

Jordan got it, much to the dismay of the White Team. Down went the starters in the exhibition game as Jordan gave them all a good lesson in basketball.

"Usually the Blue Team struggles against the White," McNairy said. "That day we beat them at everything."

Stacking Them up

He was a hotly competitive North Carolina native, a six-foot-six package of explosive energy who flew to the basket with the greatest of ease for the Tar Heels. Michael Jordan? No, Jerry Stackhouse.

Because of the above-the-rim playing style that he often employed, Stackhouse was continually being compared to Air Jordan during his time at Carolina.

As a sophomore, Stackhouse was quietly confident of his abilities. When Jordan visited the school once, Stackhouse took him on in a one-on-one contest and did pretty well by his own estimation. "I don't think he thought too shabby of me when it was over," Stackhouse said.

Stackhouse was named National College Player of the Year in 1995 and was expected to leave school early for the pros. That's what everyone was talking about when Stackhouse met with a group of reporters. He felt comfortable enough about the situation to joke about it. He said he had called everyone together "to announce that I'm going to play baseball next year."

"For the White Sox?" asked one reporter, making reference to Jordan's failed attempt at a baseball career.

"Kinston Indians," Stackhouse replied, making reference to his hometown minor-league team.

Of course, Stackhouse soon chose to forego his final two years of college for the NBA.

Left on the Court

It was January 1995, and Michael Jordan had returned to Chapel Hill for a visit. Naturally, he stopped by a Tar Heel practice to work out with the team.

Jerry Stackhouse, then considered the next Michael Jordan, spent a good part of the practice going one-on-one with "His Airness." Stackhouse decided the best thing to do was to prevent Jordan from going to his right.

After several trips down the court, Jordan said: "Jerry, I can go to my left, you know."

Making a crossover move, Jordan suddenly soared to the hoop from the left side and dumped the ball in.

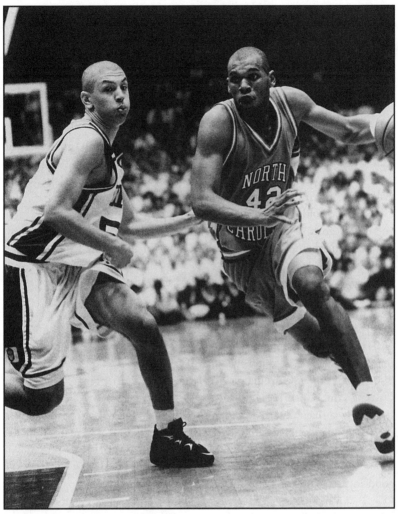

Jerry Stackhouse explodes by a Duke defender.

Just Leaving, Not Retiring from Life

Upon his retirement from coaching, Dean Smith assured reporters, friends, and well-wishers at a news conference that he would have plenty to do.

"Larry Brown [the Philadelphia 76ers coach and a former North Carolina player under Smith] has offered me a job as a janitor or something with the 76ers," Smith joked.

Of course, he could always play golf in Chapel Hill. Not every day, though.

"I'd go nutty, especially the way I'm playing," Smith said.

Actually, Smith wound up working for the University of North Carolina in an advisory capacity. The "Smith-sonian" would have to wait.

What Milestone?

Dean Smith was never a fan of cumulative records, so when the subject came up about his impending 800th victory, he pleaded ignorance.

"Where are we on that one?" he asked a reporter trying to get his reaction to the milestone number.

He was told: two more to go.

"Oh, gosh, I knew it was somewhere… because I got a wire from Billy Cunningham," Smith said. "I thought it had already happened."

Spitting in the Wind

Basketball is replete with stories about superstitious coaches. Everyone remembers Adolph Rupp and his brown suit. Or dozens of others who wore the same socks, carried a rabbit's foot, or refused to cut their hair during a winning streak.

When North Carolina played in the 1982 NCAA Final Four in New Orleans, Bill Guthridge and Roy Williams started another tradition: spitting in a river.

The two then-assistant coaches under Dean Smith, were out for a jog when they stopped and playfully spit in the Mississippi.

"We won the championship, and it became a joke that that was the good-luck charm," says sports publicist Rick Brewer.

Fast forward to 1993. New Orleans was again the scene for the Final Four, and Roy Williams was there again, this time as head coach of the Kansas Jayhawks. So were Bill Guthridge and the North Carolina Tar Heels.

For "good luck," Williams and assistant Jerry Green took the traditional morning jog, during which they spit in the Mississippi. Guthridge also ran, with Scott Montross, father of Eric. They turned down an invitation to run with Williams and Green.

Apparently, the tradition only worked for North Carolina in New Orleans. Later that day, the Tar Heels beat Kansas on their way to another NCAA title.

Defense First, Naturally

How important is defense in winning basketball championships? Ask Derrick Phelps. Or better yet, ask Nick Van Exel.

In 1993, the Tar Heels were on the road to the Final Four and looking pretty darn good—to everyone except Van Exel, the outspoken Cincinnati guard. The Bearcats were preparing to face the Tar Heels in the NCAA's East Regional finals when Van Exel spoke up, as he was known to do.

Van Exel boasted that his team was not worried about North Carolina, even though the Tar Heels had whipped a very good Arkansas team on the way to the regional finals.

For a while, it looked like Van Exel was right. He was inside, outside, and all around the court, scoring almost at will. After 15 minutes, he already had 21 points and the Bearcats had a big lead.

When the game stopped for a TV timeout, Dean Smith told Phelps to guard Van Exel exclusively. Smith ordered him to not worry about anyone else and only worry about Van Exel.

Phelps was the Tar Heels' top defensive player. Except for a tailbone injury that kept him out of the ACC championship game, the Tar Heels very well might have beaten Georgia Tech. But now he was back in top form.

He held Van Exel to just two points the rest of the way, and the Tar Heels beat Cincinnati in overtime 75-68 on their way to the NCAA championship.

George Lynch, the Tar Heels' power forward, had four great games against Arkansas, Cincinnati, Kansas, and Michigan. But everyone knew who the real star of the North Carolina team was in those playoffs.

He Should Have Kept Quiet

Any basketball coach knows you don't want to give the opposing team anything it can use for motivation. But Rick Pitino once did the favor quite unwittingly for North Carolina.

It happened in 1995 at the NCAA's Southeast Regional in Birmingham, Alabama, where Pitino's Kentucky Wildcats faced the Tar Heels in the championship game.

Rick Brewer, North Carolina's sports information director, had taken some writers out for a dinner the night before the game. In another part of the same restaurant, Pitino was also sitting with some people.

At one point, one of the writers in the North Carolina party excused himself to go to the bathroom. On the way, he overheard Pitino talking to the restaurant manager. He was making plans to reserve a room for a team "victory" dinner after the regional final.

"We told coach [Bill] Guthridge, who of course passed it on to our players," Brewer recalled.

The Tar Heels won 74-61.

They're Keepers

Practice was always sacred to Dean Smith. Getting ready for it was even more so.

"He used to spend at least an hour planning practice," remembered Rick Brewer, the Tar Heels' longtime sports information director. "He would lay out the entire practice. That was one of the most important things he did."

Smith would carry the practice schedule with him once the players hit the floor. All of the coaches had a copy of the schedule. "Here's what we're going to do: defense the first 10 minutes, offense the next 10, etc."

And Smith never threw out any of the schedules. Remarkably, he kept every last one in his office. That dated back to 1961 when he took over the head coaching job from Frank McGuire. Nobody could figure out Smith's filing system, but if he ever needed to solve a coaching problem, he had all of this valuable information at his fingertips.

High and Mighty

The Dean Smith Center starkly contrasts with Carmichael Auditorium, where the Tar Heels played their basketball games for many years. The Center, which opened in 1986, features about three times as many seats as Carmichael and attracts crowds as big as 23,000 plus.

Sitting in the top row, you're really in Blue Heaven, according to Rick Brewer.

"When I give people tickets, I tell them, 'You're in the building, but you may not be in Orange County.'"

A Tale of Two Desks

A visitor walked into the office that was shared by retired coaches Dean Smith and Bill Guthridge. Seeing that neither was in, he wanted to leave a note for Smith. There were two desks. Which was his? It would be obvious to anyone who had worked closely with Smith.

Guthridge's desk was neat and clean, everything put away in a bookshelf or in drawers. Smith's desk was the one that was cluttered with papers and folders of every imaginable kind.

"That's the way it's always been," said Rick Brewer, Smith's longtime sports information director. "Coach Smith was organized, but there was stuff everywhere. And don't you dare touch anything. He knew where everything was and didn't want anybody to disturb it."

Smith's personal "filing system" became part of his legend at Chapel Hill.

A Man of Letters

The stories about Dean Smith still answering mail in regard to his 1982 championship team may be slightly exaggerated, but they're closer to the truth than you might think.

Anyone familiar with the way he operates knows Smith personally answers every bit of mail he receives. He may or may not write the letter himself, but he reads everything that goes out under his name. He actually signs every letter, a practice at variance with many big-name coaches and athletes.

Even though he has retired, Smith still needs two secretaries to help with his mail. There's no truth to the rumor, though, that he's still answering mail from 1993 when the Tar Heels won the NCAA championship for the second time under Smith.

Their Number Was up

Keeping track of game statistics was a vital duty for Dean Smith's assistant coaches. Whenever there was a break, an assistant might walk over to the scorer's table to double-check such stats as the number of fouls on a particular player or team or the number of timeouts left for each side.

The assistants didn't want to be wrong if Smith asked "How many fouls do we have?" or "How many timeouts do they have left?"

In the 1993 NCAA Finals, North Carolina found itself in a tight battle with Michigan. The Tar Heels held a 72-71 lead when North Carolina's Pat Sullivan went to the line for a one-and-one with 20 seconds left.

Sullivan hit the first shot but missed the second, and Michigan star Chris Webber grabbed the rebound and started up court along the sidelines. That was his first mistake. He was quickly surrounded by Derrick Phelps and George Lynch, two of North Carolina's best defensive players.

Webber, standing right in front of the Michigan bench, couldn't move or pass. The only thing he could do was call a timeout. That was his second mistake.

Bill Guthridge, the Tar Heels' assistant coach, was immediately on his feet signaling technical foul. The rest of the North Carolina bench rose as well.

What did they know that Webber and Michigan didn't know? The Wolverines were out of timeouts, and a technical would be called on their bench. Donald Williams sank the two free throws for North Carolina, and the Tar Heels went on to a 77-71 victory.

"It was later said the Michigan coaching staff did not realize they were out of timeouts," North Carolina sports information director Rick Brewer said. "Our people knew. They knew that there were no timeouts left in that game for them."

Voice of the Tar Heels

It isn't often that a sportscaster stays in the same job for more than 30 years, which makes Woody Durham kind of unique.

The play-by-play man for Tar Heel basketball and football since 1971, Durham says the reason for his longevity at North Carolina has more to do with the product than anything else.

"I've had an awful lot of players make me sound good," says Durham, a North Carolina graduate who broke into broadcasting with a radio station at the age of 16.

Nevertheless, Durham's record of excellence is well known in the state. Going into the 2005-2006 season, he had been named North Carolina Sportscaster of the Year 11 times.

A Good Question

Because it was such a great example of perseverance, Woody Durham usually mentioned Carolina's spectacular comeback win over Duke in 1974 whenever he gave talks at high schools.

He had just given such a talk in Roanoke Rapids, in eastern North Carolina, when some members of the audience came up to chat. Durham noticed there was one man hanging back until the crowd thinned out. He then approached the Tar Heel broadcaster and said: "I just want to ask you something. Now who was on the floor for Carolina during that game of '74? I think you said Bobby Jones."

"That's right," Durham answered.

"76ers," said the man.

"Yeah."

"You said Mitch Kupchak."

"Yeah."

"Lakers."

"Walter Davis. Phoenix Suns."

"Yeah."

The man looked straight into Durham's eyes.

"You know what my question is: With this crowd on the floor, how in the hell did Carolina fall so far behind?"

His Way

During his many years at North Carolina, Dean Smith was generally known as a class act, whether he won or lost. Although he may not have known it, his behavior set an example for a certain LSU baseball coach.

Entering the 1991 season, Skip Bertman was still looking for his first national championship. That year, he had a pretty solid team and figured he had a good chance to win the NCAA title.

"I not only had a vision that we'd win the national championship," he said, "I had my speech rehearsed, and I knew how I'd react."

That was because Bertman had watched Smith's reaction after he won his first NCAA championship at North Carolina in 1982 and viewed Jim Valvano's win with North Carolina State in 1983.

"Smith calmly stood up, smoothed out the lapels of his jacket, straightened his tie, and walked over to shake the other coach's hand," Bertman said. "Valvano jumped out of his seat and ran around the basketball court. I thought to myself, 'There are two ways to do it.' When the time came, the Dean Smith method was right for me."

Bertman had plenty of chances to repeat the Dean Smith method. In 18 seasons at LSU, his teams won five NCAA titles.

Coast to Coast

Vince Carter and Antawn Jamison were teammates at North Carolina for three years. When both decided to leave after their junior seasons for the NBA in 1998, they made a friendly wager on who would be drafted first.

Jamison, the 1998 National Player of the Year, was picked No. 4 by the Toronto Raptors. Carter went No. 5 to Golden State.

Those affiliations were only temporary, however. Less than five minutes later, their rights were swapped. Golden State also gave Toronto cash in the deal.

"It's amazing you can go from the West Coast to the East in a matter of five minutes," Carter said.

As for that little wager between the two, Carter said, "We can call it a draw. But it's fair to say he did get drafted first. I have to give it to him."

High-Wire Act

The best dunker in Tar Heel history? You could make a case for Vince Carter. A human highlight film, the six-foot-seven guard/forward was on ESPN's "Plays of the Week" six straight weeks at one point because of his aeronautical creativity.

There was one dunk, however, that Carter wished he could have taken back. It was against Connecticut in the 1998 NCAA East Regional finals.

Carter had taken a pass at the top of the key and roared off on a fast break all by himself.

"I thought I'd do a layup," Carter said. "Then I thought, 'No, I can't do that. I'll get booed.'"

So Carter did a 360, spinning completely around in the air before slamming the ball through the basket.

Carter was pretty proud of himself until someone on the North Carolina bench said, "You did the 360 the wrong way."

Carter, it seemed, had committed the ultimate faux pas: He had rotated clockwise rather than counter-clockwise on the dunk, as he was supposed to. No matter. The reverse dunk put an exclamation point on Carolina's 75-64 victory.

"I've shown Vince a lot of films from when I played," coach Bill Guthridge joked. "I did it the right way."

Vince Carter looks to pass in one of his rare earthbound moments.

Final Word

During the 1997 NCAA playoffs, Antawn Jamison deflected questions about the possibility of leaving North Carolina for the NBA after his sophomore season.

He insisted he wasn't thinking about it during tournament time because "it's going to hurt my teammates and it's going to hurt me."

It was definitely on his mind, though, despite Jamison's vigorous denials. After the Tar Heels beat Louisville in the East Regional to advance to the Final Four, Jamison committed a Freudian slip during a news conference.

"It's every kid's dream to go to the NB—… Final Four," he said.

After which he sheepishly added, "The words just came out."

It wasn't until Jamison stayed another year at Carolina that he decided to turn pro. By then he had won National Player of the Year honors and led the Tar Heels to another Final Four.

Having a Ball

The final buzzer sounded, North Carolina had another victory, and Serge Zwikker was chasing after a loose ball. It wasn't just any ball. It was the one used during a 73-56 win over Colorado in the 1997 NCAA playoffs, Dean Smith's record 877th victory.

Zwikker, North Carolina's biggest player at seven foot three, 275 pounds, bounded across the court like a gazelle and outraced a female security guard who was also chasing after the ball. No one had ever seen Zwikker sprint that fast in practice.

Zwikker got there first. The guard tried to take the ball from the player who was practically twice her size.

"We're going to give it to him later," she said.

But Zwikker held the ball aloft, far from the guard's reach, protecting it like a piece of gold.

"No, we're going to give it to him now," he said.

Zwikker then took off for the locker room with the guard in hot pursuit. "She wanted that ball pretty bad," Zwikker said.

Not as much as Zwikker wanted it. In the locker room, Zwikker found a celebration in progress. Then he found Smith, and handed him the ball.

"Thank you very much," Smith said, beaming. "This ball represents a lot of history."

Antawn Jamison flies to the "NB—... Final Four."

Thanks to Zwikker's special delivery service, Smith didn't have to wait too long for the historic memento.

Bedtime Story

Following a coaching legend isn't the easiest job in the world, but Bill Guthridge didn't exactly fold under the pressure. In the three years following the Dean Smith era, Guthridge led the Tar Heels to the Final Four two times.

The controlled Smith was known for his sarcastic sense of humor, the genial Guthridge for his self-deprecating approach, even if it meant poking fun at his age.

One of Guthridge's favorite comments: He didn't like games that started at 9 p.m., because they kept him up past his bedtime.

From a Distance

While he was coaching, Dean Smith never felt comfortable in the spotlight. Once retired, he made sure he was even further from it.

Although still working in a consulting capacity in the North Carolina athletic department, he and his wife, Linnea, rarely attended Tar Heel games. He would only show up for games that weren't televised, or when he was asked by special request.

At home, Smith had his share of basketball, though.

Dean Smith's 877th win brought the crowd to its feet.

"I think I've got every season-ticket package or special TV feed there is," he said. "I guess I see about as much basketball now as I did years ago. Really, I probably even see a wider variety now than then."

There was another reason for staying home.

"When I get nervous at home, I can get up and walk around," he says. "It's tougher on your nerves to be a fan than to be a coach."

Three of a Different Kind

Want to known how the coaching styles of Dean Smith, Bill Guthridge, and Matt Doherty compare in a nutshell? Ask Brendan Haywood, who was recruited by Smith and played for both Guthridge and Doherty.

This is Haywood's pithy take:

"Dean Smith was more sarcastic when he wanted to get you to do something. Coach Guthridge was more laid back. Coach Doherty is more fiery and vocal when he wants you to do something and get his point across."

Profane Moment

Bill Guthridge never failed to amuse his players while coaching at North Carolina. Opposing coaches couldn't say the same.

Once during a torrid ACC game, the opposing coach wanted a midcourt meeting with referee Frank Scagliotta and Guthridge. His complaint: One of the Tar Heel players was talking to one of his players during the game.

"Frank, you've got to stop that [blankety-blank] chatter," the coach said. "That's supposed to be a technical foul this year."

Guthridge agreed to end it. At the same time he couldn't resist a parting shot.

"By the way, Frank," Guthridge told the referee, "isn't it supposed to be a technical foul this year for any use of profanity?"

CHAPTER TEN

The 2000s

Yes, you can go home again.

Roy Williams proved that legendary North Carolina author Thomas Wolfe was wrong when he coined the expression, "You can't go home again."

Not only did Williams go home, he won the NCAA basketball championship in 2005—the fourth in Tar Heel history.

It was the first for Williams, who had led his Kansas teams to the Final Four on four occasions, only to go home empty-handed each time.

Williams is a true-blue Carolinian, actually born in Wolfe's birthplace of Asheville. Williams served as an assistant to Dean Smith for 10 years before taking the head coaching job at Kansas.

In his first season as Carolina's head coach in 2003-04, Williams had modest success. The season ended in a second-round loss to Texas in the NCAA tournament.

Then in 2004-05 the Tar Heels went all the way, beating Illinois 75-70 in the finals.

The compelling 2005 playoffs were a welcome escape from the bleak news of war in Iraq and terrorism that had dominated the headlines and escalated since the September 11, 2001 attacks on America.

Welcome back, Roy. And welcome back, Tar Heels.

Carolina basketball, as guard Raymond Felton said, was "back to where it's supposed to be."

And so was Williams.

It's Still "Coach Smith" To Roy

Old habits die hard for Roy Williams.

In 2003, Williams had his Kansas basketball team in the Final Four in New Orleans. Busy as he was, he still continued a Tar Heel-related tradition he had started as an assistant under Dean Smith at North Carolina.

When he was at Carolina from 1978-88, Williams would pick up Smith's package of tickets at the Final Four so that the head man wouldn't have to wait in line.

He continued to do so, even after leaving Carolina to coach the Jayhawks. And when he came back to coach the Tar Heels in 2003, Williams was also back waiting in line for Smith at the finals.

In 2005, Williams had a bit of a problem. This time, the Tar Heels were in the Final Four and he was a busy man. Nevertheless, he still managed to secure the tickets for Smith. He sent his administrative aide, Jerod Haase, to pick up the tickets.

Dean Smith looks on as his former assistant, Roy Williams, is introduced as North Carolina's new coach. *Icon SMI*

Smith always protested, "You don't have to do that. You're no longer my assistant."

But Williams remained deferential.

"I just call it respect," Williams said.

First, After a Second Chance

In 2000, Williams was offered a job to coach North Carolina. At the time, he was the head basketball coach at Kansas.

He was torn. His roots were in Carolina. For 10 years, he was Dean Smith's assistant. But he also had a long and successful relationship with the Jayhawks.

After much painful introspection, Williams finally turned down the North Carolina job, which eventually went to Matt Doherty.

No one would have blamed anyone at Carolina if they felt Williams had betrayed the Tar Heels for rejecting the head coaching job. In some ways, Williams felt just that way himself.

Nevertheless, Williams told Kansas he would leave the Jayhawks only if he was fired or retired.

But times change.

Doherty was fired after the 2002-03 season, and Williams was again asked if he would like to coach the Tar Heels.

This time, he said yes.

Asked if he thought he had repaired any damage with his second-chance decision, Williams said, "I'm not sure that I ever can."

Well, maybe the national championship in 2005 helped to heal some of the wounds from 2000.

A Net Gain

When Roy Williams replaced beleaguered Matt Doherty as the Tar Heels' basketball coach in 2003, the new coach made believers of the players—even the players' parents.

Scott May was watching a Tar Heel practice one day and saw a definite improvement over previous years, according to his son, Sean.

"Last year he had a lot to say about the way practice was run," Sean May said of his dad, who starred on Indiana's 1976 national champions.

"But when I saw him a couple of weeks after the practice, he said, 'I have no complaints. That was one of the greatest practices I've seen from a coaching standpoint. You're in good hands.'"

One year later, of course, Williams was using those hands to help cut down the net at the Final Four in St. Louis.

Dee-fense, Dee-fense

When the Tar Heels strolled into practice at the Dean Dome early in the 2004-05 season, they had to look twice.

There were no rims on the backboards.

It wasn't a joke. The coaches wanted the team to concentrate just on defense and forget about trying to score.

"We played defense the entire practice," recalled junior point guard Raymond Felton, "just to emphasize that we don't need to score all the time to win the game."

With Felton, Rashad McCants and Sean May all back from the 2003-04 team, the Tar Heels certainly had all the scoring power they needed.

But their defense in Roy Williams's first season as head coach left a lot to be desired.

"I've never seen a bad defensive team win the national championship," Williams said, "and last year we were a bad defensive team.

"Can we change that? Will we? That remains to be seen."

Fast forward to the Final Four in St. Louis in 2005. The Tar Heels held high-powered Illinois without a point for the final two and a half minutes.

Guess the answer to Williams's question was, "Yes!"

A Big Appetite

It was game night. The Tar Heels were having their pregame meal before the national championship game against Illinois.

Some of the players were talking to Sean May about game strategy.

"Hope you're ready to eat, because we're going to be feeding you all night," they told May.

So May knew he was going to be getting the ball repeatedly in the low post that night.

May planted his large figure near the basket, and his teammates kept feeding him the ball.

The result? He scored 26 points along with 10 rebounds and was named Most Outstanding Player.

Carolina's 75-70 victory left the Tar Heels thoroughly satisfied and the Illini still hungry for the title.

A Chip off the old Hardwood

Sean May grew up suffused in the tradition of Indiana basketball. He had no choice—his father, Scott May, starred on the undefeated 1976 Hoosier team that won the national championship.

So how did Sean end up at North Carolina?

"It would have been too hard to be the second Scott May in Bloomington," Sean said. "And I knew from the way that I ate that I wouldn't be a small forward [like him] shooting jump shots."

Sean couldn't completely dismiss his heritage, though.

In tribute to his father, Sean wore the same number on his uniform (42). As a Christmas present, he had received a DVD of Indiana's victory over Michigan in the NCAA's championship game. Sean didn't watch it until the Tar Heels advanced to the title game against Illinois.

Then, "I watched it three times in two days leading up to the game."

He also showed clips to his teammates as a model of team play. He had no idea he would be seeing it again when the Tar Heels went through their warmups prior to the Illinois game.

He looked up at the Jumbotron to see his father celebrating the '76 title with Quinn Buckner.

"That really pumped me up," Sean said. "It gave me goose bumps."

Later, Sean got to do some celebrating himself when the Tar Heels won their own national championship.

He Could Never Win

From the start of the 2004-05 season, Roy Williams was set up for criticism.

This is how the thinking went: The North Carolina roster was filled with so many NBA prospects, how could Williams not win the national championship with that much talent?

"If we win it, they're going to say, 'Gosh, you're supposed to win,'" Williams said. "If you couldn't win with that group, you ain't ever going to win."

And if he lost? Williams didn't want to think about what "they" would say.

By the time the Tar Heels faced Illinois in the title game, Williams was told he had nine future NBA players on his roster–nine!

"Does that include me?" he asked with a laugh. "It must if we got up to nine."

So it was the "most talented team," vs. the "best team"—North Carolina against Illinois. Everyone knows what happened in the national championship game.

But after winning his first NCAA title, Williams was still facing criticism away from the court. This time, it was on the golf course.

"I had a hole in one," said Williams, a passionate golfer. "That's the only one I ever had. I took my wife out to the course to show her where it was.

"It was a 118-yard hole, a par-3. She said, 'Well, that's so close, that shouldn't even count.'"

Certainly a Day to Remember

During a team meeting in the fall of 2004, Roy Williams wrote a series of dates on a blackboard.

Among them was April 4, 2005, the day of the NCAA's national championship basketball game. The date had even more significance for Sean May—it was also his birthday.

"Coach, I promise you, it's going to be a very special day," May said.

Special, indeed. When May led the Tar Heels to the national title with a powerful performance, he not only gave himself a present but also gave one to Williams.

Advance Notice

Matt Doherty came to North Carolina with a well-deserved reputation as a tough coach, even though he had only been the head man for one season at Notre Dame. Actually, it took only one season to build that reputation.

Tar Heel guard Joseph Forte was part of a college all-star team with Troy Murphy, who had played for Doherty at Notre Dame. Forte wanted to know what Doherty was like.

Murphy gave him an earful. One day Doherty was so frustrated with his Fighting Irish team that he made the players run 304 consecutive sprints at practice. As a reminder of that brutal practice, some of the players wrote the number 304 on their sneakers. Not that they would ever forget.

"That got my attention," Forte said.

Bad Sightline

On the sidelines for his first coaching appearance at North Carolina, Matt Doherty seemed to be moving as quickly as his players on the court. As soon as the game started, Doherty whipped off his jacket.

The fireworks continued. Shouting and jumping, Doherty's manic coaching style was a sharp contrast to the more passsive approaches of Dean Smith and Bill Guthridge.

Doherty's players noticed.

"I try to choose a seat a couple seats away from him so I can see a little," freshman guard Adam Boone said during the 2000-2001 season.

Paradise Found

Matt Doherty's start as the North Carolina coach was nothing short of sensational. His first season featured what can easily be termed the biggest win of his young career, a wild 85-83 victory at Duke. It was the first time that any of his players had won at Cameron Indoor Stadium.

The victory stirred North Carolina students to set off bonfires and celebrations. One fan asked Doherty to autograph a homemade sign that said, "WELCOME TO THE DOHERTY ERA!"

Before boarding the bus for the short trip back to Chapel Hill, Doherty had a personal moment with his father. They hugged, and both cried.

Doherty couldn't think of much to say at the tender moment. Finally, he blurted out to his dad, "This doesn't suck, huh?"

Matt Who?

When he first took over as basketball coach at North Carolina, Matt Doherty didn't need any reminder of his relative anonymity. Sure, he played on the Tar Heels' 1982 national championship team, but 18 years had elapsed since then.

In addition, he was replacing the popular Bill Guthridge, longtime assistant to the legendary Dean Smith. Doherty, who coached one year at Notre Dame, was still trying to find his own identity.

One day early in his Carolina coaching career, Doherty was having lunch in the campus cafeteria with his wife, Kelly. A student who was sitting at the table across from them asked Doherty, "So, what do you do for a living?"

One-Upsmanship

Early in his coaching career at North Carolina, Matt Doherty discovered how tough it would be to establish himself, considering all of the success the Tar Heels had had with Dean Smith and Bill Guthridge.

Walking into the Smith Center one morning, he was stopped by a maintenance man.

"Coach, how many games do the Tar Heels play this season?"

"I guess about 35 if we go deep into the NCAAs," Doherty said.

"OK," the maintenance man said, "we expect you to win 36."

Workaholic

When he followed Bill Guthridge as North Carolina basketball coach, Matt Doherty hit the ground running. And he didn't stop. If anything, his workdays got longer throughout the season.

That didn't surprise anyone who knew the passionate Doherty, but it might have caused some reverberations at home. Asked by one reporter what surprised him about his first season as Tar Heel coach, Doherty quipped, "That my wife hasn't left me."

Nervous Time

Before coaching his first game at North Carolina, Matt Doherty had a hard time sitting still.

When the Tar Heels faced Winthrop in the opening game of the National Association of Basketball Coaches Classic at the start of the 2000-2001 season, Doherty came out with his players for warmups.

He headed for the Winthrop bench to welcome the coaching staff. Then he stood around on the court giving high-fives to some of his players. Doherty also talked with people in the stands and with others at the scorer's table.

After the Tar Heels came out with a victory, Doherty quickly got his team off the court. He didn't go into the locker room with them, however. Doherty went looking for Tulsa coach Buzz Peterson, a former Tar Heel teammate whose team was playing in the second game of the tourney. He never found him. Peterson was still in the locker room.

Later informed that Doherty was looking for him to wish him luck, Peterson said, "I hope he was OK. Before the game he was a nervous wreck. He needed to work off some of that energy."

Still Crazy After All These Years

One of the toughest places for a visiting team is Cameron Indoor Stadium, home of the Duke Blue Devils. Ask Matt Doherty, who as a player said, tongue in cheek, that Duke fans were just a group of bad-mannered Northerners from New Jersey and New York.

So Doherty, from Long Island himself, expected the worst when he brought the Tar Heels into Cameron in his first coaching visit there. And he got it.

Duke students wore T-shirts that said, "I said no to Dean." The shirt listed the names of Roy Williams, Larry Brown, George Karl, and other coaches who had rejected Smith's overtures to coach Carolina upon the retirement of Bill Guthridge.

"I think I'm sixth on the list," Doherty said at the time, "but that's all right."

Take That, Cameron Crazies

When Matt Doherty took over as North Carolina basketball coach, he put his own Tar Heel print on the program. He changed everything from the coaching staff to the seating configuration at the Dean Smith Athletic Center.

He opened up a section along one baseline for students, who used to sit up high in the 23,000-seat arena. Now up close, the vocal students could be an intimidating factor for opponents.

They were likened to the "Cameron Crazies," who make life miserable for visiting teams at Duke's Cameron Indoor Stadium. What a change from the more staid atmosphere under Dean Smith and Bill Guthridge.

The nickname for this North Carolina student section was a no-brainer—"Doherty's Disciples."

Doherty's Disciples are ready for action.

Waking up the Crowd

It was Matt Doherty's first season as the North Carolina basketball coach, but he was certainly not afraid to let his emotions show. Doherty must have set some kind of Carolina record by drawing a technical six minutes into his first game.

At halftime of one game, Doherty broke a chair in the locker room. He was also known to kick trash cans during practice.

When it came to celebrating victory, well, then he also let it all hang out. After a win over previously undefeated Wake Forest, North Carolina students stormed the court and surrounded the new coach in a spontaneous celebration, as if the team had just won the NCAA championship.

The teary-eyed Doherty went with the flow, soaking up the moment and celebrating hard along with the students. Hardly the kind of scene that would have happened with the more reserved Dean Smith or Bill Guthridge, especially during a regular-season game.

Later, Doherty told Smith, "My wife and I were talking that maybe you were looking at me in the middle of that and wondering what the heck was going on. Coach Smith said, 'No, that was great… not that I would have done it.'"

Flight of the Eagle

In the middle of North Carolina's worst basketball season in history, several former Tar Heel players returned to campus to give the team some support.

This was before the game against Florida State, a team the Tar Heels had a legitimate chance of beating. But in the miserable 2001-2002 season, nothing was a certainty.

Among the players who came back for a pregame locker room talk were Joe Brown, Bill Bunting, Dave Colescott, Jeff Denny, Kevin Madden, Ray Respess, Mike Cooke, and Al Wood.

Cooke talked about how tough it was when Dean Smith first took over a shattered program and had a losing season in his first year. Then Wood, a swingman who graduated in 1981 and was now a preacher, gave the Tar Heels his own special sermon.

He told the players a parable about the eagle that sometimes is forced to fly through storms. The eagle flies into the eye of the storm and eventually, the wind lifts the bird aloft, flying high once again.

Did the locker room talks help? They didn't hurt. North Carolina beat Florida State 95-85. Jason Capel, among others, found the visit by the former players inspirational.

"Those guys know what it's like to play at Carolina, the pride it is," said Capel, who scored 20 points as the Tar Heels won for the first time in six games. "To have those guys still be on our side shows the loyalty that comes with being a part of Carolina basketball."

The Green Monster

Every season at North Carolina, one freshman is singled out for the "honor" of carrying the Green Bag on road trips. The cumbersome bag is not taken lightly—it contains the trainer's equipment.

The player who gets the assignment is usually the most vocal of the new group.

During the 2002-03 season, it was Rashad McCants's responsibility.

About an hour after North Carolina won the Pre-Season NIT at Madison Square Garden, tournament MVP McCants came out of the locker room toting the Green Bag over his right shoulder.

Coming down the hallway at the same time was Tar Heels coach Matt Doherty.

"I can't believe you picked me to carry this," McCants said, shaking his head.

"I didn't pick you, your teammates did," Doherty said.

"It was you," McCants shot back.

"No, no. I said to everyone, 'Let's take a vote. Everyone who thinks McCants should carry the bag, raise your hand!'"

Quasi Championship

When the Tar Heels won the national title in 2005, you couldn't blame Matt Doherty for feeling he was part of it.

In fact, he was—a very big part of it.

Even though he no longer coached North Carolina, Doherty could take pride in the fact that he and his staff had recruited the key players who won the championship.

"I was proud because my staff and I put together a good team," said Doherty, talking about Sean May, Raymond Felton, Rashad McCants, David Noel, Jawad Williams, Jackie Manuel, and Melvin Scott.

Doherty laid the groundwork before he was fired after the 2002-03 season following what was described in the media as a "quasi-revolt" by players.

Roy Williams, the man who replaced Doherty in 2003, had some kind words for Doherty following the Tar Heels' victory over Illinois in the finals.

"I feel badly for Matt Doherty. Let's not forget that he was the guy who recruited most of these guys."

Doherty, who took over for Bill Guthridge in 2000, was named Coach of the Year after leading the Tar Heels to a 26-7 record in his first season. But then things began unraveling at Chapel Hill. The Tar Heels had their first losing season since 1961-62 and failed to make the NCAA playoffs for two straight years.

Exit Doherty, enter Williams.

"It was frustrating and difficult at times," Doherty said.

He had bittersweet feelings watching from New York as the Tar Heels cut down the net in the title game.

He also received a couple of bittersweet phone calls that night from former assistants Bob MacKinnon and Fred Quartlebaum.

What did they say?

"They said, 'Congratulations, we just won the national championship.'"

Now You See Him

For a big guy, Sean May was almost invisible in his freshman season at North Carolina. And so was his confidence.

He sat out 24 games because of a broken foot and even considered transferring.

Sean May grew from an invisible freshman into the star of North Carolina's 2004-05 championship team. *David Gonzales/Icon SMI*

Fortunately, he had good coaching—from his father.

"I used to tell him my first year in college was a struggle, too," remembered Scott May. "In one game, I traveled seven times!"

May told his son, "Either you're going to get better, or you're going to sit on the bench."

Good thing Sean listened to his dad.

Known as the "Cookie Monster" because of his love of same, Sean May dedicated himself to a healthier lifestyle. That included better eating habits and hitting the weights. In the next couple of years, he completely redefined his body and himself—particularly in the 2004-05 season.

The result was a big payoff for Sean and the Tar Heels in the Final Four.

Then, of course, Sean was quite visible, standing head and shoulders above everyone else as the Most Outstanding Player.

His Call

It was late in the 2003-04 season, and the Tar Heels were struggling to hold on to a shrinking lead over Maryland in the final minutes.

Suddenly, the lead looked like it was going to get smaller when the ball was knocked away from Jawad Williams with only two seconds left on the shot clock.

Then Rashad McCants stepped into the picture.

McCants picked up the loose ball, and quickly fired it at the basket. The ball banked off the backboard and dropped through the hoop.

"I was pretty open, so I just turned and shot it," McCants said.

Did he intend to bank it off the glass?

"I called glass," he said. "I did, really."

It turned out to be a game-breaker, as the Tar Heels went on to a 97-86 victory.

In the aftermath of a win, Tar Heels coach Roy Williams could poke fun at McCants for missing a breakaway dunk earlier in the half when he tried to get too fancy.

"Maybe he should have called front rim," Williams said dryly.

Sharpshooter

Roy Williams's first season as head coach of the Tar Heels in 2003-04 was both satisfying and frustrating.

The frustrating part came when the Tar Heels didn't play the kind of defense that Williams expected from his talented team. Or when they played loose and fast with the basketball, as they did against Maryland late in the season.

North Carolina led by 20 points at the half, but the big lead started to melt when the Terps forced eight quick second-half turnovers with their half-court trap.

With 4:53 left, Maryland had cut the Tar Heels' lead to merely three points.

North Carolina managed to stem the tide, and hung on for a 97-86 win. But for a while there, it was nervous time for Williams.

"You know why they don't give coaches guns?" Williams asked rhetorically. "Just watch us play."

Being Something Like Mike

When Rashad McCants was only one year old, he was already being touted as the next Michael Jordan—by his father.

In a one-line entry in Rashad's baby book, James McCants wrote: "4-12-86 next Michael Jordan."

Later when Rashad and his father met with Dean Smith, James McCants told the legendary coach that his son would be the next Michael Jordan.

It was just like a proud father. And that prediction seemed rather rash. But when Rashad scored 28 points in his first college game and set a Tar Heel freshman scoring record by averaging 17 in 2002-03, people did sit up and take notice. Jordan himself had averaged 13.5 in his first year at Carolina.

And then when McCants averaged 20 as a sophomore, same as Jordan, comparisons seemed inevitable. McCants, a six-foot-four forward/guard, didn't discourage the comparisons.

At Carolina he wore number 32 as an inverse tribute to Jordan's 23. And like Jordan, McCants left school for the NBA after his junior year.

McCants begs another Jordan comparison: a fiercely competitive nature.

"I want to see if anybody in the world can be better than Mike," McCants said. "Mike said it himself: Somebody will be greater than him. I'm not saying it's me, but I wish it was."

Well, McCants has already matched Mike with a national title at Carolina. Now all he has to do is win seven NBA championships to surpass Jordan's total.

Like Father ... Well, Almost

Talk about symmetry.

Scott May was the national player of the year when he led Indiana to the NCAA championship in 1976.

Sean May was the Most Outstanding Player when he led North Carolina to the NCAA championship in 2005.

And Sean's 26 points in the title game against Illinois exactly matched the total his father scored in Indiana's title game in 1976.

Reminded of the remarkable parallels in the NCAA title game between father and son, Sean still took a good-natured jab at his dad with this zinger:

"But he didn't have 10 rebounds."

Back From the Deep End

Winning the national championship in 2005 helped to heal some scars for Tar Heel seniors Jawad Williams, Melvin Scott, and Jackie Manuel.

It was just three years prior that they were part of a team that had the worst basketball record ever at North Carolina (8-20).

The 2001-02 season under Matt Doherty included embarrassing home defeats to Hampton and Davidson and humiliations by Duke.

"We were young," Manuel said, "and people expected us to be the saviors. But you start to understand what it takes to be a winner."

It took some time and the addition of sparkling talents like Sean May, Rashad McCants, and Raymond Felton. By the 2004-05 season, the Tar Heels had this winning thing down pat.

They finished with a 33-4 record, second highest victory total in school history.

Fresh out of North Carolina

Freshman forward Marvin Williams waited for his turn to cut down the net after Carolina's victory over Illinois in the NCAA finals. The Tar Heels' seniority system was at work.

Rashad McCants wore uniform number 32 as an inverse tribute to Michael Jordan's 23.
Like Jordan, he won a national championship while at North Carolina.

Ronald Martinez/Getty Images

It was nothing new for Williams—he had plenty of experience waiting to make his mark all season.

And he did, averaging 11.7 points coming off the bench.

"He comes in, he plays defense, he gets rebounds and he scores," Wisconsin forward Zach Morley said. "He just does whatever his team needs him to do. That's what all sixth men are supposed to do . . . come in and help the team in whatever way they can."

Although only a freshman at that, Williams's talents were widely recognized around college basketball. Before the Final Four, one broadcast analyst called Williams "the most talented player left in the tournament."

When he finally got his turn to snip the nets, Williams heard Carolina fans chanting, "Three more years."

But the six-foot-nine, 230-pound Williams wasn't listening. Shortly after the Tar Heels won the national title, he opted to go pro along with three other underclassmen—juniors Sean May, Rashad McCants, and Raymond Felton.

And after the Tar Heels' first championship since 1993, Carolina fans were left with thoughts of what might have been.

Big Shot

It was media day before the 2005 Final Four in St. Louis and Michigan State coach Tom Izzo was fretting over the upcoming game with North Carolina in the semifinals.

Talking about Carolina's extensive talent, he quipped:

"It's like, pick your poison. Which way do you want to go? Do you want lethal injection, or the electric chair?"

He wasn't far from the truth. The Spartans would eventually die at the hands of the Tar Heels.

They were actually shot to death, 87-71, as Jawad Williams pulled the trigger with 20 points.

Loosening Up

The Tar Heels were pretty loose as they approached the Final Four weekend in St. Louis.

Coach Roy Williams remembers looking out his hotel window and spotting the famous Arch and a big grassy area.

He also spotted something else.

"There were five or six of my players out there throwing a football."

Could he be sure they were actually Tar Heel basketball players, and not just a bunch of college kids tossing the ball around?

Williams could.

"I knew who they were," Williams said. "I could tell who the bad throwers and the bad catchers were."

Further or Farther?

After losing in the 2003 Finals with Kansas, Roy Williams met the press and answered dozens of questions—but very few about rumors he would be going back to North Carolina.

That had been the hottest topic as Williams prepared his Jayhawks for the Final Four.

At the end of the news conference, Williams was grateful that he didn't have to answer too many more questions on the subject.

"Thanks for not pursuing it any farther than you did," he told the media.

Standing up to walk away, Williams suddenly stopped, turned back and grabbed the microphone.

"I mean further," he said.

He was only echoing something he remembered from serving under Dean Smith many years before. The legendary Carolina coach was as strict on grammar as he was on making his points about basketball.

Williams had suddenly remembered that F-A-R measures distance.

Then he was closer to the truth.

A Monster Mash

After big victories in the 2004-05 season, the Tar Heels had made a tradition of this little postgame celebration in the locker room.

They would have a giant love fest with the players, managers and coaches mashed together, jumping and flailing around the room.

Call it the "Tar Heel Mash."

After beating Michigan State convincingly in the national semifinals in '05, Roy Williams gave his team a choice:

"We can do that jump-around thing and it will really feel good. Or we could wait until Monday (when the Tar Heels played for the national championship)."

And REALLY feel good.

The team decided to wait.

And after they won the championship?

Well, talk about a team coming together.

Back to the Future

This was after Carolina's 75-70 victory over Illinois for the 2005 national championship and Roy Williams had brought his team back to the locker room.

When they arrived, they found themselves faced with history.

No less than Michael Jordan and Dean Smith were waiting to greet them.

The Tar Heels stopped short.

"These guys are Carolina basketball," said Williams, pointing to Jordan and Smith.

Then he turned to his players, with every pair of eyes staring back at him, and delivered the message that put everything into perspective:

"But this is *your* time."

And a time it was to celebrate the continuation of the great winning tradition of Tar Heel basketball.

The torch had been passed. Smith and Jordan were there to personally hand it over.

A Tight Pair of Genes

Small wonder it is that Jawad Williams didn't wind up as a boxer instead of a basketball player

Growing up in Cleveland, Williams was given a steady diet of boxing training by his father, a onetime Golden Gloves champion.

Joe Williams coached a boxing team featuring Jawad and his older brother, Tony.

But there was another side to the family, as well. Jawad's mother, Gail, played college basketball. And his sister, Nasheema, played collegiately and professionally.

Apparently, the mother's genes were stronger than the father's.

"We couldn't get him to keep boxing," Joe Williams said. "He would be running around with his boxing gloves and bouncing a basketball."

Mistaken Identity

The car was moving along just outside Reagan National Airport in Washington when the driver suddenly stopped and pulled off to the side of the road.

He stepped out and opened the trunk of the vehicle. It looked suspicious to the security cops, who had been on alert for terrorism activities at the airport since the September 11 attacks on the United States.

Two police vehicles, their blue lights flashing, pulled up in front of the car.

The man froze. He held up his hands as the cops approached him.

They asked him what he was doing there. The man told them he was just looking in his trunk for his Official Airline Guide that lists all scheduled flights. He was hoping to catch an earlier plane.

Then one of the cops recognized the man and smiled. He held out his hand. The man dropped his.

"Congratulations," the cop said. "Good luck."

It was none other than Roy Williams, who had just been hired to coach the Tar Heels basketball team.

They Had to Hand it to Him

It was early in the 2003-04 season and the Tar Heels had gotten through five games with relatively few worrisome injuries—except one to their coach.

On the way to a rout over George Mason, the Tar Heel starters were already on the bench. Roy Williams was clapping his hands together trying to make a point to the reserves that were in the game.

After one particularly hard clap, Williams winced and started rubbing his hands.

"I clap so much that sometimes when I have that big ring on, it makes it bleed," Williams said.

He referred to a back-to-back Final Four ring that he had picked up at Kansas.

"I told these guys it's their responsibility to get me another one," Williams said.

He had to wait a year, but the Tar Heels ultimately did.

Gamesmanship

When Marvin Williams opted to turn pro after his freshman season at North Carolina, there were few raised eyebrows.

Maybe the biggest surprise was that he had actually played a year at Carolina in the first place.

"There was a lot of speculation whether he would even come to college, and you can see why," said North Carolina State coach Herb Sendek.

Sendek made the remark after the six-foot-nine, 240-pound freshman had scored 20 points and grabbed five rebounds in just 23 minutes of play against his team.

Sendek wasn't the only opposing coach impressed by Williams.

Time and again, Williams came off the bench and provided a spark for the Tar Heels during their run to the NCAA championship. He scored the decisive basket against Illinois in the title game.

"I don't think there's anything he can't do," Sendek concluded.

Well, there was one thing.

And that was?

"I can't beat Rashad [McCants] in video games," he quipped.

Things Go Better With Coke

Whenever Roy Williams talks about his childhood, inevitably the Coca Cola story comes up.

Growing up in Ashville, N.C., Williams said life was a struggle financially for his family. He couldn't even afford 10 cents for a Coke to quench his thirst after playing hours of basketball with his friends.

"I said to myself back then, 'Someday I'm going to have all the Coca Cola I want,'" Williams said.

While at Kansas, Williams once invited his high school coach to his home for a weekend. He told him to open one of his refrigerators.

It was packed from front to back with cans of Coke. And four unopened cases were also piled on top.

Don't Ask

Leading up to the Final Four in 2005, Roy Williams continued to hear the question that had popped up many times during his illustrious coaching career:

How important was it for him to win the national championship? It was starting to be annoying.

At that point, Williams was generally regarded as the best coach never to win the national title. His Kansas teams had gone to the Final Four on four occasions, only to come home empty-handed.

"I'd like to begin just one season with someone asking how many holes-in-one I had during the summer rather than how much I need to finally win a championship," he told reporters.

One-Up on Duke

How deep-seated is North Carolina's rivalry with Duke?

Well, Tar Heel fans couldn't resist the opportunity to take a friendly poke at the Blue Devils after North Carolina won the national championship in 2005.

While the Tar Heel players and their followers celebrated, some fans chanted:

"One more than Duke! One more than Duke!"

The fans, of course, referred to the total of national basketball championships accumulated by the schools. Following the win over Illinois, North Carolina had four NCAA titles to Duke's three.

And they weren't even counting the 1923-24 season when the Tar Heels went 26-0 and were declared the Helms national champions.

Sign Language

During his three years at North Carolina, Rashad McCants admittedly was a "private" person and difficult to know.

His tattoos didn't help any, either. Rashad had four words tattooed on each arm with two different mystifying thoughts.

One said, "Born to be hated." The other: "Dying to be loved."

McCants's arms weren't the only places that bore his sentiments. During the 2004-05 season, his sneakers were also adorned by many sayings and symbols.

One was a favorite scripture from the Bible:

"If God is with us, who can be against us?"

Carolina coach Roy Williams laughingly said he wasn't bothered a bit by all the writing on McCants's game sneakers—as long as "Williams RIP" never appeared on them.

Not Just Another Williams

Even though he was the third leading scorer on the Tar Heels in 2004-05, senior Jawad Williams wasn't usually mentioned in the same discussion with the team's "stars."

He wasn't even the first *Williams* mentioned. That was usually Marvin Williams, the extraordinary freshman.

But Jawad Williams nevertheless was a major force for the Tar Heels on their way to the national championship.

"From preseason he has been our most consistent player," coach Roy Williams said around the middle of the season.

How things had changed for Jawad since his freshman year in 2001-02 when he was part of a dismal 8-20 team.

Not only were the Tar Heels going through their worst season in history, Williams wasn't getting much playing time.

"It was depressing," he said. "I wanted to go back toward home and maybe transfer to Cincinnati."

His mother wouldn't hear of it. Gail Hillmon-Williams, a basketball player herself at Cleveland State, advised her son to stick to his commitment to North Carolina.

He did.

There were tough times ahead—he battled through a concussion and broken nose as a junior. But he emerged as one of the Tar Heels' most consistent players as a senior.

"Jawad is soft-spoken, lets the actions speak for themselves," said Sean May. "For that reason, he slides under the radar. People talk about Rashad [McCants], Raymond [Felton] and me."

Because of what Jawad Williams had gone through, chances are that none of the so-called "stars" appreciated the championship as much as he.

He Had a Point

It was just another average summer day for Raymond Felton—meaning he wasn't spending too much time at the beach.

He was sweating it out in a gym three times a day, practicing his shot.

Three times a day, every day—a total of 600 shots before he headed for the showers!

What had prompted Felton's fiercely dedicated workouts before his junior season?

His shooting percentage in his sophomore season—a lowly 31 percent from three-point range.

Felton hoped to dramatically improve upon that as a junior.

Coach Roy Williams wasn't happy with Felton's mechanics, which he called "technically wrong." Williams's advice: try shooting the ball with your elbow closer to your body.

Williams immediately noticed the change as the 2004-05 season progressed.

"He's got his elbow in tighter," Williams said. "It's not flying like it was last year. He's not shooting the ball across his face."

So guess what? Felton improved his three-point shooting percentage to 44. He improved his scoring average from 11.5 to 12.9. And he scored 17 points in the national championship game against Illinois, second only to Most Outstanding Player Sean May.

That included four-of-five shooting from three-point range.

The Tar Heel point guard had made his point.

On the Rebound

During his career at North Carolina, Sean May kept in close contact with his father. Win or lose, Sean would usually call his dad for a critique of his game.

And Scott May was usually very blunt.

"He's my biggest critic and my biggest fan," Sean May said during the 2004-05 season.

After scoring 24 points and grabbing 17 rebounds against Iowa State in one of his best games of the season, Sean was being interviewed. He hadn't yet had a chance to call his father.

"What's the first thing your dad is going to tell you about this game?" Sean May was asked by a reporter.

The player didn't blink an eye.

"How did you ever let that guy get 20 rebounds?," he said, referring to Iowa State center Jared Homan.

Air-Ball Jordan

For once, Michael Jordan had to take a backseat.

Jordan was on his way to Florida on a business trip early in 2005 when he stopped in Chapel Hill for a golf lesson.

While on campus, he paid a visit to a Tar Heels' basketball practice and shot some hoops with the players.

"There he was in the flesh, talking to us," recalled Melvin Scott. "Shooting around. Trying to dunk."

Jordan also participated in a half-court shooting competition, apparently not his greatest moment. First Jawad Williams sank a shot from mid-court. Then Sean May followed with another.

It took Jordan several tries before he actually made his first shot.

"All I know is I hit my shot before Michael hit his," Williams said. "I'll remember that for the rest of my life."

Three of a Kind

Charlie Everett was the third of the Everett brothers to play basketball for the Tar Heels.

Well, that might be stretching it a bit.

Joe, Jim, and Charlie all played low-profile roles at the end of the bench. Because of their limited playing time, their combined statistics at Carolina didn't add up to much.

They didn't mind. They knew that not everyone could be a star, but that a true team did need role players necessary for success: filling in for others who were injured or transferred, and serving as practice players during the Tar Heels' intense sessions.

"When I played we had [seven-footer] Brendan Haywood and [football player] Julius Peppers," Jim Everett said. "I just got killed."

Added Charlie, a senior in 2004-05:

"I never lit it up in practice or anything like that. If I don't get dunked on, it's a good day."

Conveying his Message

It didn't take long for the Tar Heels to find out about Roy Williams's competitive nature.

It was something they found out at Kansas in a hurry, too, when he was coaching there.

"He is one of the most competitive people I've ever seen," said former Kansas player Billy Thomas. "When we'd come home from road trips, he'd even want to have his bag be the first off the conveyor belt."

Give Him a Break

Intense, yes. Competitive, of course. Even a little crazy sometimes.

Roy Williams describes himself in those kinds of terms as a basketball coach.

Comparing his character traits to Dean Smith, the measuring stick by which all coaches are sized up in Tar Heel Country, Williams says he does things that the legendary basketball coach would never do.

"I'll celebrate," Williams told a reporter. "I went into the locker room (after Carolina won at Maryland) and Coach Smith would never get in the middle of a mosh pit.

"I'm not trying to say Coach Smith is an old fuddy-duddy by any means. But I do some crazy things he would never do."

Smash a clip board over his knee, for instance.

"He was in the huddle earlier this season and threw a clipboard and it didn't break," Melvin Scott said late in the 2004-05 season. "He just pounded it on his knee until it finally broke. And he said, 'This clipboard is not going to beat me.'"

Oh, well. You win some, you lose some, and some just break away.

ABOUT THE AUTHOR:

Ken Rappoport is the author of dozens of books for adults and young readers. Working for The Associated Press, he covered every major sport out of New York for 30 years and was the AP's national hockey writer for 13 years. In the 1970s Rappoport wrote *Tar Heel: North Carolina Basketball* and *Tar Heel: North Carolina Football*, detailed histories of Chapel Hill's two most successful programs.